# SPIRITUAL NAVIGATION

## FOR THE 21ST CENTURY

### SERMONS FROM WALTER THOMAS

Walter S. Thomas
Edited by Jean Alicia Elster

Judson Press
Valley Forge

**SPIRITUAL NAVIGATION FOR THE 21ST CENTURY**
Sermons from Walter Thomas

© 2000 by Judson Press, Valley Forge, PA 19482-0851
All rights reserved.

No part of this publication may be reproduced, stored in a retrieval system, or
transmitted in any form or by any means, electronic, mechanical, photocopying,
recording, or otherwise, without the prior permission of the copyright owner, except
for brief quotations included in a review of the book.

Bible quotations in this volume are from HOLY BIBLE: New International Version (NIV),
copyright © 1973, 1978, 1984, used by permission of Zondervan Bible Publishers; from
The Holy Bible, King James Version (KJV); and from the New American Standard Bible (NASB),
© 1960, 1962, 1963, 1968, 1971, 1972, 1973, 1975, 1977 by The Lockman
Foundation, used by permission.

Library of Congress Cataloging-in-Publication Data

Thomas, Walter S.
    Spiritual Navigation for the 21st Century : sermons from Walter Thomas /
Walter S. Thomas ; edited by Alicia Elster.
        p. cm.
    ISBN 0-8170-1363-6 (pbk. : alk. paper)
        1. Spiritual life–Christianity. 2. Sermons, American. I. Title: Spiritual navigation for
the twenty-first century. II. Elster, Jean Alicia. III. Title.

    BV4501.2.T482 2000
    252–dc21

                                                                                00-021969

Printed in the U.S.A.

06 05 04 03 02 01 00

10 9 8 7 6 5 4 3 2 1

# SNOWDEN

To Patricia,
Joi,
Walter Jr.,
Joshua,
and the great people of
The New Psalmist Baptist Church

# CONTENTS

# FOREWORD

EVERY SO OFTEN we are blessed to meet individuals whose unique relationship with God allows for unusual insight into the Scriptures and their application to the human predicament. One such person is Dr. Walter S. Thomas, the pastor of The New Psalmist Baptist Church in Baltimore, Maryland. He and his ministry are a phenomena in our time. How blessed we are to have in print the thinking of one whose theology and hermeneutics demonstrate what Christian ministry ought to be as we make our way in this new millennium!

Spiritual Navigation for the 21st Century is the long-awaited book by Dr. Thomas which represents prayerful study, biblical insight, pulpit genius, and a pulse on the contemporary. This volume is the work of one who takes seriously the biblical message and its timeless quest to speak to and direct Christians in our search to live abundantly and to please God. The author, a pastor, preacher, and prophet of ebony hue and experience, meets the challenge head on by concentrating on and dealing with such salient concerns as

- Overcoming the fears that grip us in this new era;
- Needing restoration when so much in our society seeks to tear us apart;
- Learning how to "let stuff go" so that we can, again, lay claim to spiritual wholeness; and
- Learning how to pursue and attain Christian ideals in a society that is content to maintain worldly mediocrity.

I commend this work to any and all people who are serious about the work of the Kingdom, who seek vision, and who are not afraid of the challenge of heretofore uncharted ministerial waters.

Rev. Dr. Charles E. Booth
Mt. Olivet Baptist Church
Columbus, Ohio

# ACKNOWLEDGMENTS

THIS BOOK WAS, INDEED, a labor of love. For years I have wanted to put into print the messages the Lord has given to me, and so many of my peers have urged me to do so. My sons and daughters in the ministry have been a great source of strength through this experience as they have sought to encourage me at every turn.

For the past twenty-five years, The New Psalmist Baptist Church has been my laboratory for preaching; that congregation has helped shape the ministry the Lord has given to me. It was a great benediction to deliver these messages among so great a people.

Deaconess Clara Major has worked by my side for over twenty years as both typist and proofreader of my messages.

This work would never have been brought to fulfillment without the able and competent assistance of Jean Alicia Elster. Her tireless efforts in keeping me on track with the schedule and in editing the manuscript have made this a work that is worthy of sharing with you.

Judson Press had confidence in an unpublished author and put their resources at our disposal to make this dream come true.

I, also, would never have been able to do this without the love and support of my favorite fans—my family. My wife and children make many sacrifices for the ministry, and I love them for every one.

Finally, my greatest and highest thanks go to God. He is at the end of the list because I wanted to save the best for last. The Lord is the joy of my life, and he has blessed me to share these words and this ministry. I can never thank him enough.

# INTRODUCTION

by Jean Alicia Elster

THERE ARE MOMENTS IN HISTORY when we, as a people, are more willing than usual to ask God to intervene in our lives. We are living in such a time, now. Even though our daily routine has not changed, and we still

- drop our children off at school;
- go to work;
- shop for groceries;
- balance the checkbook; and
- mow the lawn,

*something is different.* That difference is caused by a society that values change more than stability. Everything from cars to refrigerators to computers becomes obsolete in a matter of months. Anxiety stems from an unfamiliar global-based economy. Political instability in countries we have never heard of has an immediate impact on American life. Family life has taken new, unfamiliar, and often untried forms, and we are trying to cope with the changes. We are looking for answers, comfort, and reassurances, but none seem to be available—at least not until we turn to God. At the dawn of the twenty-first century, our spiritual lives have become the only part of our lives over which we have control.

*Spiritual Navigation for the 21st Century* provides a road map for developing the faith we will need in this new millennium. It was written to offer assurances to all seekers that God can make a way for us through these tumultuous times. It gives us a glimpse into the mighty nature of our Lord.

In this unsure, unstable age, we want to know how to grab onto the promises of God while steering clear of the pitfalls and distractions that stand ready to block our spiritual progress. We want to look at what we believe and then plan our way, follow a course, and position our lives in this new era. We want to know how to be spiritually ready for the challenges that could upset our souls and steal our joy. Christians and skeptics alike want to know, "What does the Lord have to say about *my* life?"

This book helps us look within ourselves to find the answers; it helps us look at our faith to find the answers; and it helps us seek the face of God for our answers.

# 1

# SERIOUS BUSINESS

In the past God spoke to our forefathers through the prophets at
many times and in various ways, but in these last days he has
spoken to us by his Son.... We must pay more careful attention,
therefore, to what we have heard, so that we do not drift away.

—*Hebrews 1:1–2; 2:1, NIV*

## PROMISE OF THE TWENTY-FIRST CENTURY

THE CLOSING CHAPTERS of the twentieth century brought us
many significant and sometimes startling new trends. The past one
hundred years saw the movement of society from an agricultural
base to an industrial complex, from horse-drawn carriages to
horsepower-driven automobiles. We watched industry rise and fall.
We saw the captains of industry become rich and wealthy while our
urban centers matured and decayed. Yet, as the century wound to
a close, the major topic was not the demands of labor and the
strength of management but the rise and expansion of the infor-
mation "superhighway." Computers, e-mail, and online services
exposed us to a larger and more complex world than Laura Ingalls
Wilder ever dreamed of living in her *Little House on the Prairie* or
John Boy Walton ever conceived of on "Walton's Mountain."

Having entered a new millennium, we can stand in a mall or on
any major city street and watch as people march by with their ears
almost attached to their cellular phones. They are able, in a matter
of moments, to be connected with distant parts of the world while

paying for a pair of running shoes at the sporting-goods store. Modern humanity is pushing buttons that stretch even the wildest imaginations. Life has become a complex interaction of networks that link the diverse and the divergent into one nebulous system. There is the Internet, the cellular net, the cable net, and what can be called the "hood" net. One cannot be a citizen of this era without feeling the pull of events, technologies, and new trends. The twentieth century already seems like ancient history and the time immediately before that almost prehistoric. The video rendering of the Josephine Baker story ends with her singing a song written by Bob Dylan that so appropriately describes what we are seeing—"The Times They Are A'Changing." This new millennium is as good a time as any to stop, take a good look within ourselves, and take stock of our lives.

Even as we begin this inward journey, the Lord has made this promise to us: We will not have to traverse this uncharted territory alone. This is made clear in Hebrews 1:1–2 *(NIV)*. The writer of the Book of Hebrews begins this missive with the flat-out statement that God is speaking to us through his Son. God is ordering the conversation; he has selected the medium; and he has declared, decreed, and directed the message. In former times, God spoke through prophets and others, but now (and the now is still now) he is speaking to the whole of humanity through his Son. The Creator is doing the talking. He is talking to us through the revelation of his Son, and we are to do the listening and the heeding. In other words, we are not to try to make God fit into *our* order: He is calling us, through *his* Son, to fit into *his* world and *his* kingdom. We are the recipients of this major word from God. Culture changes from period to period, but Jesus Christ is the same yesterday, today, and tomorrow.

This is how Christ makes good on his promise "Lo, I am with you always, even to the end of the age" *(Matthew 28:20, NASB)*. He fulfills this by sending into our lives the Holy Spirit, the Comforter, the Counselor, the believer's friend, the Paraclete, the third person of the Trinity. God has put a portion of himself into each and every one of us, and that is serious business! Christ has supplied us with his spirit. He has filled the void in our lives, the tank of our soul, and the reservoir of our humanity with something other than this world. He has filled us with the very essence and substance of himself, and we must be careful how we handle what he has given us. You see, when we accept Jesus Christ as Lord, something more than walking down an aisle takes place. Jesus Christ, the Savior of humanity, puts some of himself in us so that we will have his presence with us always.

If you are—
- still getting high,
- still running the streets,
- still lying and jiving,
- still with one foot in the church and one in the world,
- still falling by the forces of life,

then remember that God has put a portion of himself in you, and he is no one to play with. He came into your life and mine to give us something greater than anything we could ever imagine. We must be serious about our desire to rise, fly, turn around, and go somewhere, because he has given us all the equipment we need to accomplish what must be done.

There is another promise that the Lord has made to us: The Holy Spirit not only equips, but he also *reveals*. That is why we must be serious. The work of the Holy Spirit is to reveal to us and for us what we would not see on our own. Some of us have almost gone to war with the Spirit because he was showing us what we did not want to see. But that is exactly why Christ sent him to us. We cannot reach our potential or accomplish his work without true spiritual vision. We must see behind the scenes and have revealed to us what is deeply disguised. The Holy Spirit tears the covers off this world!

He was sent from Christ with a specific mission to show and keep us in the truth. We must not let the lies of this world cause us to dismiss the truth and revelation that the Spirit brings. There is a wonderful passage in 1 John that says, "test the spirits to see

**3**

whether they are from God" *(1 John 4:1, NIV)*. The supply of power that has been given to us is spiritual. This is serious work, because those false, alien spirits are out to destroy and dismantle the work that God is doing in us and through us. Listen to the word of God:

> I tell you the truth: It is for your good that I am going away. Unless I go away, the Counselor will not come to you; but if I go, I will send him to you. When he comes, he will convict the world of guilt in regard to sin and righteousness and judgment: in regard to sin, because men do not believe in me; in regard to righteousness, because I am going to the Father, where you can see me no longer; and in regard to judgment, because the prince of this world now stands condemned.
>
> *John 16:7–11, NIV*

## PITFALLS OF THE TWENTY-FIRST CENTURY

While God stands at the door, encouraging us to heed the Word that is spoken through his Son, there are what might be called new paradigms emerging around us. Life is not what it used to be, by any stretch of the imagination. Just as the ground shifts in the first few seconds of an earthquake, the tremors are now being felt in our own lives. Society is encouraging us to change our expectations of what is good and acceptable. While cottage industries and home-based offices are becoming more prevalent—allowing segments of the workforce to enjoy increased flexibility in lifestyle—they are evolving in such a way that people can work in their homes and never see those for whom or with whom they work. Isolation is becoming the norm.

Individually, we have gone through other transitions. We do not want to wait for anything; we want life on demand. From hamburgers to homes, we want to acquire everything quickly. Instant happiness is our requirement. We think about "me, myself, and I" and have found a way to live without a community. We have become self-absorbed and impatient. What we call progress is being taken too far.

In our so-called religious life, there are many things that we have let slip because we are not guarding them or valuing them enough. There was a time when we taught our children to pray when they ate a meal and before going to bed, but we have let that slip. There was a time when we were regular in our church attendance and gave our tithes and offerings, but we have let that slip. There was a time when we sought God for everything and trusted him to provide our daily needs, but we have let that slip. When we let these things slip, we see and feel God's power, purpose, productivity, patience, and peace flow right out of our lives.

Even in our worship services, we want to be entertained and hear a message that fits comfortably into our daily existence. We shy away from being convicted; we hide from being challenged. In essence, we want a religious elixir that will make us feel good!

Tragically, the pitfall here is that we have tried to make God fit into this new world order. God—

- the Alpha and the Omega,
- architect of the universe,
- keeper of time, and
- the convener of eternity—

is being asked to conform to our agenda and our way of living. This is a dangerous and risky course of action because, any way you look at it, we are the losers. It is dangerous to try to make the Lord conform to us. We were made in his image, not he in ours. Even though our world has changed and is still changing, we need to understand one very important thing: When we talk about our relationship with God, it is serious business! Christ is the standard, and his standards are higher than those of any culture.

One of the mistakes we often make is in confusing Christianity with culture. That was the mistake of previous centuries when Western societies called the cultures of foreign nations "heathen" and "barbaric" and saw their own as "Christian" and "cultured."

In our new era we have gone full circle—we have defined culture as the authority and seek to make our faith conform to it. We must not forget that culture is but a medium and Christ is the mediator. Culture is impersonal, but Christ is our personal Savior!

## ADVENT OF THE TWENTY-FIRST CENTURY

As we said earlier, the Lord's standards are high and the challenge is for us to rise up and meet them. This is a major challenge because there are some things we have to let go, renounce, give up, and turn away from if we are going to stand firm as Christ's disciples in this new millennium. We cannot treat him as we do other things. We must reject the theories of the dominant age and conform to his world.

Paul's words in Romans 12:2 should never be taken lightly: "Do not conform any longer to the pattern of this world, but be transformed by the renewing of your mind" *(NIV)*.

These words call us to understand the high standard and the high calling that is upon our lives. There is something more important than getting that promotion, buying our dream house, getting over the heartbreak, surfing the Internet, or updating our wardrobe. Jesus commands us

- to love
- to maintain our joy in him
- to walk in peace
- to be gentle
- to suffer for righteousness
- to proclaim his Word
- to be light in the darkness
- to bear one another's burden.

This requires serious commitment. Our Lord is not asking for a halfhearted pledge to try to do better. He wants an everyday, every hour commitment to be the people he calls us to be. We have to stop fooling ourselves. We can get a good feeling on Sunday at church when we listen to the choir, but better still that we rejoice at the voice of wisdom that comes from the Lord. We can get excited about the message of a good sermon, but we should feel our spiritual cup running over when we receive a revelation from on high and use that power to accomplish the plan the heavenly Father has shown to us. Commitment is a high standard, and we should never diminish it!

But something happens when we start to talk about commitment. People get nervous. People feel confined. They say they want their freedom. They even mention free will. Those people do not understand that freedom is never without responsibility and commitment. We must be committed to something; we must live as if our lives depend on something, and that something is Jesus Christ.

What about those whose commitment is not to the Lord? Jesus' response in Matthew 25 is clear. The Master will say, "Depart from me.... For I was hungry and you gave me nothing to eat, I was thirsty and you gave me nothing to drink ... I was sick and in prison, you did not look after me" *(vv. 41–43, NIV)*. It is for this very reason that our commitment is essential. An army with unreliable soldiers is a disaster waiting to happen. That is why the military takes its raw recruits and puts them in basic training—they can then be forged into a fighting force to be reckoned with. In the same way, the Lord wants us, his army, to become a force to be reckoned with.

That is why the Master instructed his disciples to abide in his Word. That is why Paul said, "... be steadfast, immovable, always abounding in the work of the Lord ..." *(1 Corinthians 15:58, NASB)*. Be committed! Get serious, stop drifting, and get dedicated. If we are truly serious about this business of doing the Lord's work, then we will sing hymns and psalms; lift our voices in prayer; serve both in and out of season; help where we are needed; be convicted by the Word; be inspired by the truth; worship and praise without watching the clock; give him all honor and glory; work at becoming more than we already are. We will fight the good fight; keep the faith; finish the race; stand for the truth; and carry the name of Jesus throughout the twenty-first century!

# 2

# OVERCOMING FEAR

When the seventh month came and the Israelites had settled in
their towns, the people assembled as one man in Jerusalem. Then
Jeshua son of Jozadak and his fellow priests and Zerubbabel son of
Shealtiel and his associates began to build the altar of the God of
Israel to sacrifice burnt offerings on it, in accordance with what is
written in the Law of Moses the man of God. Despite their fear of
the peoples around them, they built the altar on its foundation and
sacrificed burnt offerings on it to the Lord, both the morning and
evening sacrifices. Then in accordance with what is written, they
celebrated the Feast of Tabernacles with the required number of
burnt offerings prescribed for each day. After that, they presented
the regular burnt offerings, the New Moon sacrifices and the
sacrifices for all the appointed sacred feasts of the Lord, as well
as those brought as freewill offerings to the Lord.

*—Ezra 3:1–5, NIV*

## PROMISE OF THE TWENTY-FIRST CENTURY

GOD IS OFFERING US the opportunity to experience a new
vitality in this twenty-first century. It is a vitality—a renewed energy—that will touch every fiber of our being and every aspect of our
lives. Nothing—not our spirituality, nor our intellect, nor our emotions—will escape the power of this vigor. As we move onward,
this vitality will give us a life-affirming, invigorating freedom from
something that has crippled and immobilized us in the past: fear.

Fear has both a positive and a negative side. *The American Heritage Dictionary* defines fear as "an emotion of alarm and agitation caused by the expectation or realization of danger." This emotion can, obviously, do us a great deal of good. If we are walking down a secluded, quiet nature trail and suddenly a giant grizzly bear crosses our path, fear becomes a method of self-preservation when a sudden rush of adrenaline enters our muscles and allows us to outrun and "out climb" this giant creature. A knowledge of the rules of food preparation and a fear of the consequences of food poisoning cause us to prepare our food properly and store it at the correct temperature. These are healthy fears that promote our safety and well-being.

The problem arises when our fears become unrealistic and irrational. We fear:

- the advance of years as we grow older,
- the impermanence of our current job,
- the dissolution of a longtime, serious relationship,
- the breakdown of our health,
- the future of our children.

These are just a few of the "pitfalls" of the new millennium that we will examine shortly. These unhealthy fears can disable us and create such havoc within our lives that we cannot see the mighty promise of freedom from fear that the Lord is holding out to us. As a response to this negative side of fear, this promise of the new millennium offers hope. Our new millennium is not a time to wait and see, to cringe in a corner, or to wish instead of act. Freedom comes from a direct confrontation with the destructive fears that live and lurk within us. We can banish those fears, face them on their own ground, and decisively defeat them.

This promise of freedom from fear declares that fear is not to be our controller. We are to walk by faith, letting faith conquer the fears we have. Although President Franklin D. Roosevelt encouraged our nation in a time of war by asserting that "we have nothing to fear but fear itself," the tent maker from Tarsus put it best when he wrote, "For God hath not given us the spirit of fear; but of power, and of love, and of a sound mind" *(2 Timothy 1:7, KJV)*. The spirit of fear that tries to make itself at home in our personality was not given to us by God. He gave us love, power, and self-discipline. Fear is inconsistent with these potent attributes from God. Love, power, and self-discipline are the resources most necessary to negotiate life. God put them at our disposal so that we would not have to listen to fear. Do not have any doubt, God will make good on his promise; he intends for us to overcome fear. We will see just how the Lord will prepare us to take hold of this promise. But right now, we need to look once more at the text from the Book of Ezra as it lays out another important truth that we must address about this life-changing promise.

"Then Jeshua son of Jozadak and his fellow priests and Zerubbabel son of Shealtiel and his associates began to build the altar of the God of Israel to sacrifice burnt offerings on it, in accordance with what is written in the Law of Moses the man of God" *(Ezra 3:2, NIV)*.

The fears of the people were overcome because those who were spiritual took the lead! Jeshua the priest and Zerubbabel the governor took the lead. They mobilized the workers. They organized the effort. They gave the word. Leadership is the call and the demand of this new age.

More than that, the twenty-first century sounds a call for *spiritual* leadership. The Lord has blessed our intellectual capabilities to the extent that we can connect with anyone at anytime at anyplace on the planet by just pushing a few buttons on our computer. We have new responsibilities to take the lead to reach these same people and guide them on the path of freedom from the encumbrances of fear. Those who would be leaders must challenge the system and enable people to move from the point of fear to the point of freedom. They must be like Moses leading the children of Israel from bondage to freedom. They must be like David leading the people into a new sense of community. They must be like Jesus leading the world from sin to salvation. When we take the lead, the promise can work through us to the point of fulfillment.

The church needs to hear a special word for the twenty-first century. The church cannot close ranks and retreat into its beautiful sanctuaries without regard to those still struggling in the world. The church must take a leadership role in bringing people to the possibilities that exist for them. The church must accept its role as leader. It must challenge its own fears and march forward, picking up those who need a push. The church has a job, and that job is to help others overcome their fears.

The Scriptures teach us that the strong must bear the infirmities of the weak. This is not a popular teaching in our day and time when many churches have become obsessed with their own glory. They look good because everything around them looks so bad. Our communities, our families, our jobs, and our lives are crumbling while churches are rejoicing in their own glory. The church is not called to be beautiful; it is called to make the world beautiful. The church is called to bring people from their darkness into the marvelous light. That requires that the church take the lead, regardless of the cost.

Whether by the work of individuals or by the work of the church, fear's power can be broken through the power of Jesus Christ. He has given us the power of his Spirit so we can face whatever seeks to deter our development and, with grace and dignity, rise above it all. Christ empowers us to face our fears and face them down. Fear cannot stand against a steady onslaught of Word, faith, praise, trust, and commitment. Though we may fear the battle because we fear the outcome, when we stand on the battlefields of life with our sword in hand and our armor before us, the victory is ours. Christ has already won the battle.

## PITFALLS OF THE TWENTY-FIRST CENTURY

It is important to take a closer look at some of these fears—these pitfalls—in order to gain a better understanding of what we are battling against. It goes without saying that one of the strongest emotions in the human soul is fear. Psychology teaches us that the two strongest emotions are not, as we like to believe, love and hate, but rather love and fear. Fear can march into our psyche and suspend the advance of ideas and activities. Fear can raise concerns and issues that may sabotage all our progress and all our plans. Though fear is a reality that we have confronted in the past and still must confront, we have let it become an all-encompassing force within our lives.

You name it, and we have a fear to accompany it. The effects of fear can overtake us even before we realize what has happened. We move from slight concern to stark terror. We move from something simple, such as the fear of breaking a mirror, to the horror of being afraid to leave the house. We move from taking precautions against the crime that may exist in our neighborhood to being afraid to go to an evening church program. We are afraid that we will not pass a test, that our marriage will fail, that we will not get a promised promotion.

Each of us has our own fears that, time and time again, get out of hand. We become overwhelmed by the dark side of our thinking, and we dread the next thought that bubbles to the surface for our consideration. Therapists and counselors are finding their appointment books filled with patients who are under the domination of their own fears. These unwelcome guests can move into our minds and then refuse to leave! They come to take charge. Positive suggestions by spouses, family, and friends are met with responses such as, "I would, but you don't understand."

- I *would* go back to school and get my degree, but you don't understand how hard it would be to go to work, come home and feed the family, go back out to class …
- I *would* stand up to my drug-addicted son and tell him he's either got to get clean or get out of the house, but he might come back and trash the place or smash the windows of my car …
- I *would* stop hanging out at the singles bar on Friday nights and start going to Bible study, but there aren't many single people at my church and I'm not getting any younger ….

The age in which we live does not work to alleviate this sense of terror. We fear what power the forces of negativity have in our lives. We are terrified of the influence and the strength that the ungodly seem to possess. Every day there is one more thing to worry about—the drug use epidemic, crime, racism, sexism, political scandal, computer viruses, stock market crashes, droughts, famines, floods. The list can become overwhelming. Our capacity to worry is reaching its limit, and our ability to take on new concerns has almost been extinguished. In the words of Old Testament scholar Walter Brueggemann, people have lost their ability to articulate their pain, are incapable of an in-depth critique of the modern culture, and are in dire need of creative responses that liberate and inspire hope.

We are struggling with life itself. In fact, sometimes it seems as if we are not the victors at all but rather the victims. We are more guided by our fears and concerns than by the saving truth of God that we know and have learned to hold dear. Fear has become a major player in the game of life. Yet there is a way around these disabling pitfalls; there is a way out. We *can* lift ourselves and others above the forces and fears that have held us captive for so long. The Lord has prepared a way for us to accomplish just that.

## ADVENT OF THE TWENTY-FIRST CENTURY

The Bible works to equip us to overcome fear. In fact, in our text from Ezra, we see God doing that exact thing with the people of Israel. For nearly seventy years, the children of Abraham lived in the cities of Babylon. They made their home in a strange land and sought the Lord about their release. They had made their beds hard, and now they were being forced to lie in them. The people of the land held them in low esteem, and their homeland was but a memory. It seemed as if their captivity would never end. Just when they had about given up, God stepped in and made a way out of no way.

Never count God out! He *will* step in and make changes take place. He will restore. He will do as we read in Ephesians 3:20 *(NASB)*, "exceeding abundantly beyond all that we ask or think, according to the power that works within us." What happened to the people of Israel? Cyrus, King of Persia, gave the decree that they could return home. Under the leadership of Jeshua the priest and Zerubbabel the governor, they went back to the land of promise.

It is important to note that when the children of Abraham were taken captive, her captors repopulated the land of Israel with foreigners. These foreigners intermarried with the sprinkling of Jews who were left behind and became known as the Samaritans. Other tribes conquered by the Assyrians, the Babylonians, the Medes, and the Persians were also brought to this land to live. They occupied the land while Israel was held in captivity, and they felt as if the land were now theirs. These new inhabitants did not take kindly to this group of Jews returning to Jerusalem, claiming their heritage, and seeking to reestablish their customs. They knew the land and were well trained and well prepared to face this new generation of Jews returning to claim it as their home.

It goes without saying that the children of Israel were afraid. The text makes it clear that they feared for their lives. They were afraid of a people who hated and disavowed their God. What caused them to overcome their fear? They overcame it because their fear of God was greater than their fear of the people who inhabited their land.

## Reverence and Respect

It is important to note that in this instance "fear of God" means reverence and respect. Their reverence and respect were greater than their anxiety about the consequences that would befall them. Their veneration for God was greater than their vulnerability. They loved the Lord. They knew how far he had brought them and how much he meant to them. This text teaches us that we must spend time venerating God and loving him for who he is in our lives. Then we will be able to look at our fears and say, "You can't make me doubt him; I know too much about him."

Knowing God for who he is encourages us and empowers us to go forward, even when our fears are screaming an alarm. Moses must have welcomed that solitary moment with God when he stood at the banks of the Red Sea and heard God speak. That conversation allowed him to stretch out his rod and see the waters divide. As with Moses, reverence for God will empower us more than we realize. We will recognize the power that he has exercised on our behalf. We can take note of the various victories that have been ours and the struggles that he has successfully brought us through.

One of the reasons morning prayer time is so important is because it allows us to reverence God, adore God, glorify him, and magnify his name not only to heaven but, more importantly, to ourselves. We start the day realizing how important he is and how much he means to us. It is out of our reverence for him that we can accept the call to challenge our fears and be confident that their demise is eminent.

## Worship

It goes without saying that the children of Israel were afraid of the people who inhabited their land. The text makes it clear they feared for their lives, yet as Jews there were certain things they had to do. They had to maintain the Torah; they had to honor the rite of circumcision; they had to make regular sacrifices to God. They had to worship. We still hold this in common with the people of Israel. We have to worship. We cannot escape that truth. Being Christian defines us as being worshipers. We have to make a joyful noise and lift a word of thanksgiving to him. Regardless of circumstances and situations, something inside us cries out to honor the God we love and adore.

Jeshua, Zerubbabel, and their fellow priests and associates "began to build the altar of the God of Israel to sacrifice burnt offerings on it, in accordance with what is written in the Law of Moses.... Despite their fear of the peoples around them, they built the altar on its foundation and sacrificed burnt offerings on it to the Lord, both the morning and evening sacrifices.... they celebrated the Feast of Tabernacles ... the regular burnt offerings, the New Moon sacrifices and the sacrifices for all the appointed sacred feasts ... as well as ... freewill offerings to the Lord" *(Ezra 3:2–5, NIV).*

In spite of all they were dealing with, they built the altar in order to make sacrifices to the Lord. They challenged their fears and gave their gifts to God, not once, not twice, but numerous times, and nothing adverse happened. The enemy did not overtake them. The enemy did not even come looking for them. The children of Israel took a leap of faith and, in doing so, learned how to overcome fear. In the providence of God, true worship is never separated from the work of liberation. When we really worship God and adore him, he compels us to move forward—freeing us from our fears—to finish what he has commanded us to do in our lives.

## Spiritual Leadership

As we mentioned earlier, the text in Ezra 3:2 teaches us an important truth: Spiritual people have a responsibility to help lead others in the path that they should travel. We cannot be uninvolved. Just as Jeshua and Zerubbabel took the lead, we are called as the body of Christ to lead his people to the promised land.

When the children of Israel prepared to enter the Promised Land, the priests and the Levites were out in front. When they marched around the walls of Jericho, the spiritual leaders were out in front. When David brought the ark back to Jerusalem, they were out in front. Spirituality forces us into leadership positions. Someone is waiting for the brother or the sister who knows God to tell them that they can conquer the mountains in their way. We hear these calls, but we turn a deaf ear because we believe we have other more pressing duties. There is no more pressing duty than that of liberation.

The priest and the Levite taught this lesson in the story of the man on the road to Jericho. They had other business to attend to and could not stop to help the man who lay dying on the side of the road. They thought their other work took precedence over serving. Today there are many churches and church leaders who do not have time for the man on the road. They are on their way to praise

God, whom they have never seen, while ignoring their brother, whom they see every day! The Bible is still true when it says, "faith without works is dead" *(James 2:20, KJV)*. Our society is afraid: afraid of outsiders and afraid of itself. The church must go forward with its spirit of compassion and declare by example that it is possible to overcome every force that seeks to hinder us.

The history of the civil rights movement leaps up to support this claim. We are indebted to people such as Sojourner Truth, Harriet Tubman, Denmark Vesey, David Walker, and so many others who put their lives on the line to lead a great number of enslaved Americans from bondage. They realized that those who have seen the light and who have, through the power of God, been set free from the very forces that are still laying siege, have an obligation to go back and bring others to the glorious light of liberty. Where would we be if it had not been for those churches that dared to believe that their God was standing with them in the struggle and refused to back down in the face of terror, lynchings, and burnings? The church took leadership, and because of its sanctified warriors who pushed past their fears and acted upon their faith, we have open housing, open education, voting rights, and open accommodations.

Spiritual people cannot surrender leadership to fretful and fearful people. Someone must stand and declare, "The Lord will make a way somehow."

## Challenge and Overcome

The final emphasis of the text is found in verse 3: "Despite their fear of the peoples around them, they built the altar on its foundation and sacrificed burnt offerings on it to the Lord, both the morning and evening sacrifices."

Despite their fear they built their altar, assembled the people, and offered their sacrifices. The text does not say they offered the required sacrifices once and said, "That's enough!" It says they offered the sacrifices one after another. They offered the New Moon sacrifices, the sacrifices for all of the appointed feasts, and the sacrifices that were brought as freewill offerings to the Lord.

They did not challenge their fears once and then say, "I'd better not push it." The people of Israel challenged their fears until their fears could no longer stand. They challenged their fears until fear's power over them was broken. They continued to offer sacrifices, aware that the people of the neighboring areas were watching and threatening. They trusted in their God and sacrificed once, twice, and three times on into the next day and the day after that and the day after that. As they continued to sacrifice, they no longer considered the possibility and the power of their own fears.

We have to challenge what has been planted in our hearts and minds and realize that God is leading us toward something major. Had the children of Israel not faced this fear and accepted this challenge, they would not have rebuilt the temple. They would not have prepared themselves for the coming of the Messiah. By challenging their fears, they opened the doors for greater blessings to be theirs and for greater heights to be reached. One victory led to another.

By this example, we must overcome fear and let the power of the Spirit guide and direct us. Our troubles can be turned into triumphs. If we take one step, God will take two. He will take the steps if we challenge the conditions. He will bring us out and restore our journey. On the day of Pentecost, Peter challenged his fear by declaring the gospel of Jesus Christ. Three thousand souls were added to the ranks that day. Peter faced one fear after another until city after city was converted and town after town came to Christ. We do not have to wait until God raptures his church; we can trust him now and defeat the fears that hold us back. It is time to trust, try, and triumph. The Lord has promised, and it will come to pass.

# 3

# PUSH ON!

Don't let anyone look down on you because you are young, but set an example for the believers in speech, in life, in love, in faith and in purity. Until I come, devote yourself to the public reading of Scripture, to preaching and to teaching. Do not neglect your gift, which was given you through a prophetic message when the body of elders laid their hands on you. Be diligent in these matters; give yourself wholly to them, so that everyone may see your progress. Watch your life and doctrine closely. Persevere in them, because if you do, you will save both yourself and your hearers.

—*1 Timothy 4:12–16*, NIV

## PROMISE OF THE TWENTY-FIRST CENTURY

ONE OF THE DOUBTS that rightly dances into our consciousness is expressed by the question, *How high can I really fly?* We watch those who are proficient at their craft and competent in their profession, and then we step back and wonder not only how good we ourselves are at what we do but also how much better we can become. It is neither unnatural nor uncommon to consider one's abilities and then look at the heights that might actually be accomplished. How many times have we watched others and then said to ourselves, "I can do that"? What we can and cannot do is a serious question. We do not want to be exiled to the barren territory of our inabilities; instead, we want to rise to heights that we know are possible.

R. Kelly, a popular recording artist, penned a song that echoed through the souls of listeners across the globe: "I believe I can fly. I believe I can touch the sky."

Most of us want to believe we can fly and that we, too, can touch the sky. Michael Jordan has made the dream come true. Oprah Winfrey has broken the paradigm. The internationally renowned neurosurgeon Dr. Ben Carson has explored the far reaches of his profession. It can be done. It has been done. It will continue to be done. Many of us can still remember our youthful dreams and our visions of the future. We would be the Lone Ranger, Zorro, Flash Gordon, and Superman all rolled into one. My mother used to tell me when I was just a youth, "Dream as high as the heavens; then if you miss, you won't feel bad landing on a cloud." The point here is an admonition to dream big, and the bigger the dream the better.

The message that is needed in this day and time is one that calls us to push on! If we are to negotiate this new millennium, we must find the resolve, push beyond the obstacles, and rise above the barriers to make things happen. The twenty-first century has its own unique share of pressures, as well as new and challenging realities. If we do not have a mind-set of accomplishment, we will be lost in the rising tide of complex concerns.

For us to have this mind-set of being able to do what we set out to do, we have to accept one very basic truth: We are fully equipped to accomplish all things when Christ is in our life. Too many of us do not realize how much is rightfully ours by virtue of being members of the family of God. In the opening Scripture of this chapter, Paul does not speak to Timothy as if he is lacking in anything. In fact, he takes the opposite position and says that Timothy must not neglect the gift that he has. In Christ, Timothy is fully equipped to do the work he was appointed to do.

Consider David. He looked so ill-equipped for his battle with Goliath. Even the prophet Daniel appeared to be no match for the powers of Babylon. Our Savior Jesus looked like a guppy in an ocean of pharisaic sharks. In each and every case, the Lord's people came out the victors. In each case, they believed in the skills, talents, and gifts they had to offer. In each case, they cried out, as in Romans 8:31, "If God be for us, who can be against us?" *(KJV)*.

Our background, our upbringing, our intellect, and our social position are not the determiners of our success. The gift that Timothy had, the gift given to every believer, is the Holy Spirit. The Spirit is there to equip us with every resource we need to reach our divinely appointed goals. The power of the Holy Spirit leads us into battle, sustains us in the crisis, and then elevates us in victory. This gift of God offers us the power to challenge the status quo of life and make the impossible happen.

In this advent of the new millennium, we must start seeing ourselves as real children of God, rightfully heirs and joint heirs of Jesus. As the world progresses and life becomes more complicated, God offers us more and more strength, power, and wisdom. When we accept these gifts, when we are faithful to his calling, we are blessed. Paul did not need to wait until he died to know that he had the favor of God. In his trials and in his efforts, he learned that he had the favor of the Almighty. It was after his struggles that Paul heard the Lord say, "Well done."

Look at any success you may have had in your life or any accomplishments you may have realized. The Lord made it happen! He is with you and wants you to use your gifts so that you can rise up as an even greater witness and let your life speak his praise. In other words, "… let your light shine before men, that they may see your good deeds and praise your Father in heaven" *(Matthew 5:16, NIV)*.

## PITFALLS OF THE NEW MILLENNIUM

Many of us start out with big dreams, but the dreams seem to end up as nightmares. We start the race with a bang and end it with a whimper. Something comes along to short-circuit our dreams and make us settle into a mediocre reality. For some, the American dream has been filed away in the library of life, serving only as a reference book to be occasionally taken from the shelf. For others, the significance of being African American has been all but lost and little or no value is placed on how far we, as a people, have come; instead, emphasis is placed on how far we have to go. Many have recalculated what it will cost to become the person they desire to be and concluded the costs are too great and the goals will never be attained. They have cashed in their chips and left the table. They do not believe that the doors to their dreams will open as easily in their lives as they have opened for others.

This is more than an attitude or a tendency. A problem we face as we negotiate our way within this new millennium is that the ethic of struggle and success has been replaced with an ethic of complacency and marginality. We have lost our drive and are willing to do whatever we have to do just to get by. There was a day when we struggled against all odds to make a life and to make life work. Those days seem to be gone. A job is a job, a house is a house, a life is a life, and a marriage is a marriage. We have lost the adjectives and yet we still feel the sentence is proper without them.

This is a spirit of complacency. This is a directing of thoughts and energies that leads people to accept defeat and give in to their less-than-desirable situations. There is a spirit at work here that causes people to settle for things the way they are and makes them concede before they conquer. There is a force at work that has lulled so many to sleep and caused them to accept whatever comes, giving up on the dreams God helped them to have.

Some people have given up because the struggle has just become too hard. They tire of the constant struggle and the uphill battle. Their ship did not come in and has not been spotted from the light-house. Some have given up because they have incorrectly evaluated themselves and concluded they are no match for what may lie ahead. They have used a life formula that failed to properly account for the contribution that God will make whenever we first put forth the effort. They have failed to remember that God never leaves us to accomplish any task completely on our own or solely with our own abilities. He steps in and makes the difference.

Some people have given up their dreams for a reason we hate to state publicly: They are lazy. They do not feel like putting in the time or the energy needed to get the desired results. They prefer the pleasures of a season for the favor of a lifetime. They are shallow about the future and knee deep in the present. They have not given themselves to hard work. They are lazy. Many of us have seen it in others and had it identified in ourselves. There is an old song of the church, written by Isaac Watts, that is relegated to revivals but that ought to be sung on a daily basis to revive us.

> Am I a soldier of the cross,
> A foll'wer of the Lamb,
> And shall I fear to own His cause,
> Or blush to speak His name?
>
> Must I be carried to the skies
> On flowery beds of ease,
> While others fought to win the prize,
> And sailed thro' bloody seas?
>
> Sure I must fight if I would reign;
> Increase my courage, Lord.
> I'll bear the toil, endure the pain,
> Supported by Thy word.[1]

Somehow we must reverse this tide! We must give our young people a knowledge of purpose and drive, our young adults a sense of direction, our older adults a feeling of excitement. With the challenges of this new millennium all around us, we cannot sit back and let life pass us by. We must rise up and meet the challenge. The world may be content to be complacent, but the church must remember that it is militant and engaged in a truceless battle. We cannot allow ourselves to be complacent. Too much is at stake. In both our personal and public lives, we must push ahead.

The other week I walked through the halls of our church's school and watched the little children as they made their way to class. I thought to myself that they will have so much to master and so much to learn in order to compete in this age. What kind of models do they have in this world? We have so many in our society who have copped out. Educators struggle to have our youngsters accept the pabulum of education. Drug dealers present an alternative lifestyle, telling our youngsters they cannot survive in the major leagues and inviting them to take part in the minor league of genocide within their own community. We need to give our youngsters a godly witness. Look at every area of your life and know that it is a witness. Rise up to the challenge and win because you represent the Lord Jesus Christ. Paul tells Timothy to stir up that gift and use it so he can accomplish the work God has assigned to him. He says this to Timothy because he wants his young friend to realize that God will hold him accountable for the work assigned!

## ADVENT OF THE TWENTY-FIRST CENTURY

I noticed this truth while scanning the letter Paul wrote to his young ministry friend, Timothy: Here was a man at the end of his journey, writing to one at the very beginning of his. Here is age addressing youth, reality addressing potential, the "been there" addressing the "on the way." Paul was nearing the end of a marvelous ministry. He had carried the name of Christ to the far-flung reaches of the empire. He had set up the cross as the premier emblem of worship. He had established colonies of faith in the bastions of heathenism and polytheism. He had caused Caesar's followers to forsake the eagle for the lamb. Letters that bore his signature were read in the churches, and miracles had been done that taught faith and opened eyes. His had been an illustrious career, lifting up the name of Jesus. Peter had the ministry to the Jews, but Paul had succeeded in his efforts with the Gentiles. He had an understanding and an appreciation for hard work. He had crisscrossed the world three times, been shipwrecked, beaten, and jailed. But each time he pushed on and persevered, accomplishing his goal. He later wrote in 2 Timothy 4:7, "I have fought the good fight, I have finished the race, I have kept the faith" *(NIV)*.

He ran into obstacles at each twist and turn in the road. He was forced to escape in a basket over the wall of Damascus. He found persecutors in Thessalonica, Athens, and Corinth. The Philippians beat him and put him in the bottom of the jail. He had his detractors, and there were those who wanted his work stopped and his life ended, but they did not stop his effort or dissuade him from his cause. His career carried with it the marks of great pain and suffering.

With little time left in his hourglass, Paul wrote to his young friend and gave him a powerful word of instruction. Paul was not naive. He knew that this young man did not have an easy road ahead of him. He was aware that the chances of survival were slim since the Jews used Roman law to cripple and kill those who followed Jesus. Timothy would have many forces working against him, and he would have more than one reason to abandon the work and return to the home place of his family. Indeed, Paul had not forgotten that "Demas, because he loved this world, has deserted me and has gone to Thessalonica" *(2 Timothy 4:10, NIV)*. Timothy's youth would be, for some, a hindrance. His association with Paul would anger others. There was much he must deal with if he was to be a leader, if he was to "push on."

Timothy, for his part, had seen Paul rise above every challenge. He had marveled at Paul's ability to face life and come out victorious. He had desired to be able to use that same strength in his own situations. He had seen it modeled, but it was something else to try to make it happen in his own life. Timothy was now in the driver's seat. Without the proper focus, one of three conditions could exist:

- success could spoil him and cause him to settle into an arrogant ministry;
- failure could overwhelm him and cause him to end his work and cease his efforts; or
- he could just limp along, accepting whatever came his way.

Knowing this, the apostle told his young friend that he must uphold the high calling that was his. He must not allow others to look down on him because of his youth. He must preach and teach. He must go forward. Paul admonished Timothy, "Do not neglect your gift, which was given you through a prophetic message when the body of elders laid their hands on you" *(1 Timothy 4:14,* NIV). In his second letter to Timothy, Paul put it more succinctly by telling Timothy to "stir up" the gift that was within him. In other words, Paul was saying, "You have something within you that will empower you to overcome anything and everything that is in your path. Push on, because you have what you need!"

Paul is also speaking to us today. We must not judge ourselves by our background or our circumstances. We must look at who we are and trust the power and presence of God in our lives to give us the victory. Many times we live off our defeat because we do not know how to allow the power of the Spirit to give us victory. We must not shackle ourselves because of prior failures; God has and will give us the victory. In order to move in this power of the Spirit, we must believe that he is at work in us. He will work through us even when we do not feel worthy. He will do so because he wants us to see the love of God at work on our behalf, thereby proving that "no weapon that is formed against you shall prosper" *(Isaiah 54:17,* NASB).

It is not time to quit; it is time to face what we have always wanted to accomplish and know that God has equipped us to get there. Stop letting dreams die because we are willing to accept another reality. We have within us the person of the Holy Spirit, and he will empower us!

This may sound like unfamiliar territory, but that is not the case. All we have to do is say, "Lead me, Lord," and the Spirit will do the rest. It is our responsibility to trust him and follow his lead. Remember the words of Hebrews 11:6, "… anyone who comes to [God] must believe that he exists and that he rewards those who earnestly seek him" (NIV).

When I was a child, my father saw it as his responsibility to push us whenever we wanted to quit. I have adopted the same mind-set with my children. I know that quitters never win and winners never quit. I want them to push themselves as far as they can go.

Our struggle is our witness. What melts us at Calvary is the Christ who will not quit. He will not be broken; he will not surrender. He pushed himself to the very brink. I am drawn to him not only by his words, but by his efforts. If we are going to change a generation and turn around a people, we must show them that they, too, can push on. The gospel is about our witness. Jesus told his disciples that they would be his witnesses. Regardless of what else we are, Christ commands us to be his witnesses. We are to reveal him to others. He is the Unconquerable Christ. He can rise above every situation and defeat every foe. That is what God wants us to show the world. We cannot, like the man in the parable, build our barns and sit back while life goes on. We must do more, conquer more, and overcome whatever stands in our path. It is in our victory that others see Christ. If he is real in our lives, then he will be real in the lives of others. We must challenge systems and situations. We must be the Lord's army.

Many of us do not realize that God is not just giving assignments; he has a purpose, he wants a work done, and he is confident that we are capable. He will hold us accountable for the work assigned. God will hold us accountable for the blessings we should have received and the witness we should have made. He will empower, and he wants us to move on. He will strengthen us. The new age demands a new vigilance. We must not back down or give ground. We must sound the battle cry, "Charge!" The songs of our parents must be revived. We cannot let complacency become the order of the day. A *new* day has dawned, a *new* hour has come, and the people of God have to rise to the challenge.

*Defeat* is a word we must push out of our vocabulary. There is too much at stake. Our families, our children, our friends, and our God need to see that we are a determined people. We do not have to give up. It is not essential that we collapse. We can push on and keep climbing. God has a destination for us, and we cannot stop until we reach it. When we do reach that destination, we will have elevated his kingdom's cause and taken his people to a new level. We must stand and sing, as our parents did, "I'm on the battlefield for my Lord; And I promised Him that I would serve Him till I die. I'm on the battlefield for my Lord."[2]

Let us continue to "push on" and meet the challenge!

---

## Notes

1. *"Am I a Soldier of the Cross?" Words by Isaac Watts. Reprinted in Gospel Pearls (Nashville: Sunday School Publishing Board, National Baptist Convention, U.S.A., 1921), 48.*
2. *"I Am on the Battlefield for My Lord." Words by Sylvana Bell and E. V. Banks. Reprinted in The New National Baptist Hymnal (Nashville: National Baptist Publishing Board, 1977), 493.*

# 4

# REJECTION OR RESTORATION?

Brothers, if someone is caught in a sin, you who are spiritual should restore him gently. But watch yourself, or you also may be tempted. Carry each other's burdens, and in this way you will fulfill the law of Christ. If anyone thinks he is something when he is nothing, he deceives himself.

—*Galatians 6:1–3,* NIV

## PROMISE OF THE TWENTY-FIRST CENTURY

ON AUGUST 8, 1974, Richard Milhous Nixon resigned as president of the United States. The House of Representatives was headed toward passage of a bill of impeachment that would have summoned him to stand trial before the Senate, with the Chief Justice of the Supreme Court as judge, while the charge of high crimes and misdemeanors was aired before the American people. Nixon chose to escape such a historic confrontation. He had been involved in the infamous cover-up of the break-in of the Democratic national headquarters in the Watergate Hotel. The Plumbers—a covert operations unit set up in the White House to gather intelligence—had bungled its operation, and the president was caught in the midst of the ensuing scandal. Richard Nixon became the first president of the country to resign.

It was a dark day for American politics. A sitting president relinquished his role as leader of the free world because of his own offensive activity and his knowledge of the devious behavior of his underlings. In fact, many people went to trial and many lives and careers were destroyed. Some of these same people are just now beginning to resurface and reshape their lives. This was not America's finest hour.

Watergate, as this scandal was quickly dubbed, was more than a historical event; it reshaped the way Americans view government, people, and life. It smashed our rose-colored glasses and caused us to look for the devious and deceptive in everything that happens. Though *Washington Post* journalists Woodward and Bernstein did some of the century's best investigative reporting in bringing the Watergate scandal to light, they opened Pandora's box and caused every journalist since that day to look for the cover-up and seek to be known for the scoop.

In government, scandal has become the order of the day. Since Watergate, other incidents in our nation's capital have included Koreagate, the Iran Contra scandal, President Clinton's "Monicagate," and the accompanying barrage of special prosecutors. The stamina of many of our political leaders is put to the test on a daily basis.

On our jobs, employees are asked to spy on other workers. Everywhere we turn, someone is under investigation for something. Every day some new revelation costs someone his or her livelihood and future; some mistake becomes paramount and dismissal follows. From industry to individual relationships, we have come to the point where we are governed by suspicion and where there is absolutely no room for mistakes.

This is not to say that justice must be hung out to dry and we must excuse every mistake and gloss over every indiscretion. God forbid! However, true justice understands the role of mercy. "Good people" make mistakes and sin like anyone else. No one is exempt from the madness that has infected our world. The Bible puts it best: "… for all have sinned and fall short of the glory of God" *(Romans 3:23, NIV)*. There are some reading these words who have struggled to do right but made one mistake and lost their good name, their family, their livelihood, and their self-respect. Even the perception of wrong can be so damaging as to do irreparable harm to the person who is falsely accused.

What is a person to do? Are we to be like F. Scott Fitzgerald's main character in *The Great Gatsby* and head out for parts unknown? If mistakes disqualify us from the race, then why go on living? The answer is clear: We go on living because the world is wrong. There is life after a collapse. There is life after failure. The great promise that holds true even in this new millennium is that there is grace for the journey!

From the time that he walked upon this earth, Jesus has brought into our midst a new community, and it is his desire that all people be welcomed into it. His method is to restore and not to reject. The New Testament message is one of restoration after mistakes so that we can regain our place in society. The role of the community of the redeemed is to restore those who have fallen and help them regain their footing. The message of faith from those of us who claim that the Spirit of God guides and governs our lives is that there is grace and restoration. This is the call of the gospel.

The Christian doctrine of grace says that God knows we are prone to fall and that we make mistakes. It goes on to announce that God still loves us and has given us grace to reestablish—restore—our relationship with him. Grace is the backbone of the gospel because it declares that God has given us his unmerited favor. We did not deserve it, and we could never earn it, yet our repentant approach to his throne by our confession of sins causes him to "forgive us our sins, and to cleanse us from all unrighteousness" *(1 John 1:9, KJV)*.

Jesus will sustain our efforts and, in the process, restore his people. Examples from the Bible bear this out:

- Zacchaeus, the tax collector, was an outcast of the community. He was a publican, among the lowest in society, yet Jesus gave him back his life and his hope. He restored him to fellowship.
- The lepers were outcast and forced to live in a separate community. No one had dealings with them for fear that they, too, might become unclean. Yet Jesus spoke to them, touched them, healed them, and restored them to the community.

- There was a man, possessed by a legion of demons, who lived in the tombs and ran wild. He was rejected by society and often chained because he was an annoyance. Jesus met the man and mended him. He took the demons away and gave the man deliverance. Jesus took his brokenness and gave him blessedness, took his hurt and gave him hope.

We can bear witness to this truth. There have been times when we were absolutely guilty and the world was ready to write us off, but in the heavenly realms, Christ stood up on our behalf and interceded for us. We were taken off the hit list and put on the healing list. Some of us know that we have been given a second and a third chance because the Lord is concerned about our becoming better. He is not rejecting us. By his grace, he is restoring us.

## PITFALLS OF THE TWENTY-FIRST CENTURY

Even with this knowledge of grace, one of the major pitfalls still with us in the twenty-first century is that we are obsessed with mistakes. We are concerned with what people do wrong. We fire them, jail them, ostracize them, and reject them. We have not healed from deep hurts and terrible wounds. We have not recovered from our own experiences with broken trust and misplaced loyalty. We now act as if everyone must suffer! We have no program for restoration. We have no plan for rebuilding the lives of the fallen. We have no desire to help those who have fallen by the wayside. We let our wounds guide our lives.

Two thousand years ago Jesus Christ set before us teachings and principles that could carry us safely into *any* millennium, yet we have chosen to move beyond his imperatives to do unto others as we would have them do to us and to forgive those that sin against us. We have ignored his model of rescuing people who are their own worst enemies. We have decided that we want no part of the sinner or the fallen person. We want to be both judge and jury, and we want to see those accused pay dearly for their transgressions.

Our human side is never indecisive about its response to a wrong suffered. It wants an eye for an eye. It wants to banish the infidel. It wants payment for injustice. We see it every day. People are in court for everything, looking to collect damages as if money were the answer to every hurt. We want someone to suffer for the crimes, mistakes, and failures that have intruded on our lives and caused us grief. We want to see them hurt and watch them struggle with pain so they will know how we felt. If we cannot get to the person responsible for our deepest hurt, we take our dissatisfaction out on others. We have national scapegoats, local scapegoats, and personal scapegoats.

Even the attribute of mercy has become strained in our society. On the night of the 1988 presidential election, the various networks ran all-night commentaries on the reason for the defeat of Democratic Party candidate Michael Dukakis. Most of the speakers concluded that Dukakis' answer in one of the campaign debates to the hypothetical question of the rape of his wife was not the response expected by the American people. One of the commentators said Mr. Dukakis lost because he did not realize that the American people want revenge!

However, the gospel calls us to a new level. It calls us to let the new life in us deal with the trouble that is around us. This is difficult because there is a war going on within us. Perhaps that is what Paul meant when he said, "There is a war going on within my members, when I would do right evil is present" *(Romans 7:23, paraphrased)*. Evil wants us to renounce what God is saying and let our anger boil until we don the robe of the jurist, pass sentence, and strike the gavel, declaring that the case is now closed. God is looking for repentance; we are looking for revenge.

## ADVENT OF THE TWENTY-FIRST CENTURY

We must return to what God says about the faults and failures of people. We must assert that there is a fundamental distinction and a foundational difference between the way the people of God handle mistakes and the way the world deals with them. The God response is the one the church needs to champion as we negotiate our way through this new millennium. We must move beyond the quest for the perfect person and deal with the imperfect people in our midst and in our lives. The world would have us believe that we have to choose between crime and punishment, but there is another way. We must reject the choice and declare that a new model is necessary. We must move from rejection to restoration!

Paul, the tent maker from Tarsus, gives us a glimpse into the mind and method of God. The region of Galatia needed a word. The Jewish believers were there pushing their brand of Christianity. They were teaching the new converts that since Jesus was a Jew, everyone who came into the faith had to adhere to the covenants that guided Judaism. They preached circumcision, Sabbath worship, and adherence to the Torah. These practices would have defined them for all the world as followers of Jesus and members of the Jewish faith, but Paul understood that the circumcision God wants is of the heart. God does not want practices where there is no deep spiritual fervor.

Moreover, Jewish law was very rigid concerning the sins and the mistakes of others. The Old Testament laid down immutable responses to certain indiscretions and made as hard as bedrock the belief in "an eye for an eye." There was little, if any, room for grace. This is the context in which Paul wrote his advice in Galatians 6:1–3. He did not want the new community of believers to get off on the wrong foot. He wanted them to be in line with the will of God, and so he cautioned them about how to handle someone who had obviously made a mistake.

Paul told the church of Galatia that if someone was caught in a sin, those who are spiritual should restore the one who made the mistake. This is the demand of the Lord. We must model his behavior and seek to bring people into fellowship. Our society rejects and repudiates those who make mistakes, but the Kingdom is about restoration.

One of the great New Testament lessons is contained in the story of the woman caught in the act of adultery. There was no doubt that she was guilty. The crowd brought her to the Master to be judged, but he turned the tables on them and demanded that they judge themselves first and, based on their judgment of themselves, *then* judge the woman. Jesus said to the crowd, "Look at yourselves, and, if you are free from mistakes, pass sentence on the woman" *(John 8:7, author's translation)*. In other words, only those who are without sin have the right to judge others. Since the only one who fits that category is the Master, he alone can declare the end of the matter. Jesus looked at the woman and asked, "Where are those thine accusers?" He continued, "Neither do I condemn thee: go, and sin no more" *(John 8:10–11, KJV)*.

Jesus' word gave the woman an opportunity, and that opportunity gave her back her life. He modeled what the Kingdom is all about. The Kingdom is about restoration, not rejection!

There are those who will take exception to this position. They will ask, "How can we say that only those without sin can pass judgment? That is ludicrous, because everyone has made some mistake. What, then, is the purpose of law? Is not law given to assure that those who commit infractions are removed from the community?" Such a view runs contrary to the purpose that Jesus lifts up. One of the lessons of Galatians 6:1–3 is that it is God's plan for people to become better, but it is the responsibility of the redeemed to make this happen. Paul says, "… you who are spiritual …" In other words, those of us who are in Christ have to let our spiritual nature govern our actions. The text teaches that the real weight is not on the shoulders of the one who has made the mistake but on the shoulders of the one who must respond. This is an alien concept for us, but if we are to survive in this new millennium with its proclivity toward mistakes, we must embrace a new paradigm. This is without a doubt a hard saying. However, it is the call of the gospel.

Some time ago, Dr. Kortwright Davis of Howard Divinity School posited a great thought. He spoke about the South African response to its holocaust and the Jewish response to its holocaust. All of us are well acquainted with both. The Jews were nearly wiped out by Adolf Hitler. Death on an unprecedented scale defined his era. Brutality under the guise of science cost many their lives. Apartheid denied a race its rights and left it at the mercy of a minority who saw no value in its existence. Thousands were killed and tortured; the true story will never be fully known.

Dr. Davis compared the two responses. The response to the Jewish Holocaust was the Nuremberg Trials and the continued hunting of Nazi war criminals, that they might be brought to justice. It was an appropriate response for that day and that era. It was the best that the world had to offer with so many nations being accomplices to Hitler's genocide. The South African response has been the Truth and Reconciliation Committee, which has offered amnesty to the oppressors and tried to bring healing to a fractured land. To some this may look weak, but it is the call of the gospel. We must seek to be reconciled with those who have caused us pain. It does not matter if that pain is directed toward us or has just entered our space. We must seek to restore the one who has fallen.

Scripture says, "How can you love God whom you have never seen and hate your brother whom you see everyday?" *(1 John 4:20, paraphrased)*. This is our question. If we are spiritual, then we must be led by the Spirit of God, who fears no future and is not bound by any past. We can restore because no situation really has complete sway over us. We can be agents of restoration because, as Paul said to the Romans, "In all these things we are more than conquerors.... [Nothing shall] separate us from the love of God that is in Christ Jesus our Lord" *(Romans 8:37–39, NIV)*. The weight is on us. We must put up or shut up. This is the mark of being spiritual.

We have something special, and we need not be afraid to use it to strengthen others. We have been given a great gift. We have the presence of the Spirit of God, and that Spirit can enable others to discover the power that is in their lives. The song says, "They will know we are Christians by our love." It is our love that constrains us and makes us want to sow into the lives of others the seeds of wholeness and blessing.

In Galatians 6:1, the word Paul uses for "restore" is a word that means to mend. There is another word for restore that means to restore to a former condition of health, but that word is not being used here. In this text, Paul speaks of mending a body part, a dislocated member of the body. He is, in essence, saying that this person is a part of us but has become dislocated. Somehow the person became separated from the joint and must be mended. This is always the case with dislocation. Dislocation is the result of believing a lie that Satan plants in our minds and then spreads throughout our spiritual system. The aim of this action of Satan is that we will become so involved in the life that the lie produces that we will ultimately turn away from God. The lie is about our self-worth. It weds itself to all our unresolved issues. It cuts through the tissue of our uncertainty and attaches itself to all our fears. It drives like a crazy person. It tells us we cannot change and that we are evil. It tells us we are fallen and we will never be right. It convinces us that there is no hope for our condition. It fine tunes our weaknesses to a perfect pitch and then plays us like a violin. It knows where to attack and what to attack with. We become so absorbed in our pleasure and pain that we have little time or use for God. That little lie has the destructive power to dislocate us from the body.

This is why the spiritual have to go to work. Our job is to help people renounce the lie and mend. Paul told the church at Ephesus that "our struggle is not against flesh and blood ..." *(Ephesians 6:12, NIV)*, and no truer statement has ever been made. We fight against a force that is subversive, covert, and disguised. We cannot allow those who belong to the world community to just dangle. They must be mended!

During my youth, there were often stray dogs rummaging through the neighborhood. There was a wooded area not far away, and many of these dogs lived there. We called them "ghetto dogs." Many of them were hopping on their front or back paws because one foot was damaged. Some dogs lived for years crippled with broken limbs and dislocated members. They were forced to live that way because they had no master. There was no one to take them to the veterinarian and help mend their broken bones. God has declared that we cannot be like these ghetto dogs, limping through life, dragging fallen brothers and sisters, and leaving them in their crippled state, unable to fulfill their function. He says we must restore those crippled members and bring them back into the body by way of healing and deliverance.

It is interesting to note that the tense of the verb Paul uses when he says "restore" is called the continuous present tense. This means that the action is not completed by one deed but is ongoing and continuous. We must be "restoring" that person. This is where it gets rough, because this requires patience and perseverance. We have to be willing to work with our brothers and sisters, aware that Rome was not built in a day and that it will take time to get the lie out of their system and have the truth birthed and matured in them. We must take time with people and know that God is about the process of their restoration and the process of their deliverance.

This is why Paul adds the word of caution in that same verse: "But watch yourself, or you also may be tempted" *(Galatians 6:1, NIV)*. During the mending time, we have to be in proximity to the mess in others' lives. We cannot help people if we are standing afar; we must get close to them, as Jesus did. We must touch the leper, speak to the sinner, fellowship with the outsider, reach out to the addict, counsel the offender, and stand alongside the corrupt. This is dangerous ground, because the forces of evil are there in assembly, but remember, "Greater is he that is in you, than he that is in the world" *(1 John 4:4, KJV)*. We cannot face this fight alone, because our anger allows us to be compromised by the evil we face.

It is for this cause that we were born. We were put here to bring forth a better world. We are here to help others find their way back to the path of life. We are here to announce that there is a new plan. We may not succeed in every case, but we must understand that our charge is not to reject but to restore. The knowledge that we have of our faith and the clear call of the God we love cause us to find a more excellent way to reach out to others. God will sustain our efforts and, in the process, restore his people.

# 5

# LET IT GO!

Therefore I tell you, do not worry about your life, what you will eat
or drink; or about your body, what you will wear. Is not life more
important than food, and the body more important than clothes?

Look at the birds of the air; they do not sow or reap or store away
in barns, and yet your heavenly Father feeds them. Are you not
much more valuable than they? Who of you by worrying can add a
single hour to his life? And why do you worry about clothes? See
how the lilies of the field grow. They do not labor or spin. Yet I tell
you that not even Solomon in all his splendor was dressed like one
of these.

If that is how God clothes the grass of the field, which is here
today and tomorrow is thrown into the fire, will he not much more
clothe you, O you of little faith? So do not worry, saying, "What shall
we eat?" or "What shall we drink?" or "What shall we wear?" For
the pagans run after these things, and your heavenly Father knows
that you need them. But seek first his kingdom and his
righteousness, and all these things will be given to you as well.
Therefore do not worry about tomorrow, for tomorrow will worry
about itself. Each day has enough trouble of its own.

*—Matthew 6:25-34, NIV*

## PROMISE OF THE TWENTY-FIRST CENTURY

IN 1984, OUR CHURCH bought its first computer, an Apple
IIe. This was our introduction into the computer age. Prior to

this, our phones were five-button sets with a hold button; we prepared the Sunday bulletin using a Selectric typewriter, duplicating stencils, and a mimeograph machine. When we purchased our computer, we entered the technological age. We brought the church into the modern age. We found a way to increase our productivity and cut down on the work we had to do. As the years passed, we upgraded the systems, changed the telephones, and added pagers, cell phones, printers, and other high-tech devices. We now have expanded our capabilities to include the Internet, radio, and television.

The promise of the twenty-first century was that all this new technology would enable us to do our work in less time and thereby give us more free time. We would be able to fulfill ourselves because our time would not be filling us. Computers replaced manual operations and, in theory, decreased the amount of human hours needed to do a task. That part has come true. The problem, however, has come from the fact that we have *added* functions, tasks, and assignments to this free time. Downtime is now a thing of the past. On planes, on trains, and in restaurants—nearly everywhere and anywhere—people are working nonstop, trying to stay ahead of the game.

Some years ago, the state of Maryland followed suit with other states and repealed its blue laws, which had made it illegal for large businesses to operate on Sundays. Sunday was seen as a day of rest and a day set aside for family. The proponents of the repeal of the laws said that those who worked in businesses that chose to be open on Sunday would not be *required* to work, and the repeal would not cause Sunday to be just like Monday. How wrong they were! Malls and markets are buzzing on Sundays, and employees are required to work their appointed shift. There is little difference between Sunday and Monday.

What have all these changes done for us or, rather, done *to* us? Have they made the quality of life that much better? Have they liberated us from the struggle of everyday life and given us the peace— the nirvana—that we desired and anticipated in those early days?

Has a drop in the rate of heart attacks and strokes accompanied the four-day workweek and flex-time schedules? Have we become less tense and more tolerant? Has the pressure in the cooker of life dissipated? The answer to these questions is a resounding no! In fact, stress-related illnesses are on the rise. Families are falling apart at an alarming rate. People work all the time and live in terrible fear of the future. Social scientists now speak of the unemployed, the underemployed, and the working worried. The working worried have a job but no peace. They worry about their permanence in the workplace. They worry about being dismissed if their productivity falls. They worry about downsizing and right sizing. They worry that their company will be sold and their job reassigned.

We cannot handle the volatility that life has produced. The stock market can, with its wild roller-coaster swings, wipe out wealth in just one day. The merger mania and the emphasis on the bottom line can have employees so troubled that enjoyment of work and labor become a thing of the past. Attempts by the government—both local and national—to decrease regulations have not brought any solace. The legal system can bankrupt us, the health-care system can decimate our finances, and the prospect of growing old in a loving, caring environment is becoming increasingly remote.

Though we call ourselves a health conscious society and do everything we think we need to do to stay healthy, excess fat is killing us, and obesity has been identified as one of our number-one plagues. Why? Because these are by-products of a system that has us sitting all day, working all week, and taking little recreational time. Pharmaceutical companies are hurriedly pushing new drugs through the Federal Drug Administration approval process just to meet the demand for their stress-reducing benefits. It almost seems as if the world is popping pill after pill to handle a myriad of stress-related problems. Simply put, the race has become too much for us; our attempts to alleviate the stress are having little or no effect. The pace is too fast, the demands are too numerous, the pressures are too great, and the stakes are just way too high. We cannot keep up.

Families are suffering as children try to grow up in this pressure cooker. Friendships are no longer nurturing, they are professional. We are about to explode, not just as individuals, but as a race, a nation, and as a civilization. We need some measure of stability, something we can hold on to as an anchor. As we size up our place in the twenty-first century, we must decide whether we will be run by life or whether life will be run by us. We have to decide what is important and what is not, and then we have to let some things go.

The text from Matthew 6:25–34 is from the morning of the Master's ministry. He had not been on the scene long, and he was setting the stage and laying the groundwork for the methods he would use to conduct his ministry. One of the lessons we should all learn about the Master is that everything he does is for a reason. His methods and his message speak clearly, and people can hear, see, and understand what he is trying to teach. He came to give us eternal life, and in order to accomplish it, he had to combat the prevailing notions about this earthly life.

Though their technology was far inferior to ours, the stressors of life during Jesus' day were very present and extremely powerful. They held a certain sway over people and, as such, they made life difficult for many. The Romans had conquered their nation and established garrisons within their territories. Tribute was extorted by publicans—the tax collectors—and soldiers stood ready to handle the slightest infraction of the rules. The possibility of freedom was less than remote. Theirs was a world where "hope unborn had died." They were a conquered people.

The religious stressors of that day were just as potent. Zealots plotted the overthrow of Rome, Sadducees affirmed the status quo, and Pharisees condemned the masses for their failure to keep the jot and tittle of the law. There was little about which to rejoice.

Even the disciples who followed Jesus were caught up in the stress that controlled their lives. Some were fishermen, one was a tax collector, one was a snob, and two were sons of a local entrepreneur. They did not have much, and their prospects for improvement were limited.

Some things do not change from era to era, generation to generation, or millennium to millennium. The desires for "the good life," with nice things, a future, prosperity, good health, and the like, are constants and claim the thoughts and attention of every generation. They are the goals of a comfortable life, and they have propelled every society and undergirded the ethos of every era.

In his Sermon on the Mount, Jesus pointed out a very important reality. The people were striving for these goals but not reaching them. They were obsessed by a quest they could not seem to fulfill. They worried about life but could not change their reality. Their inability to make a difference was destroying the inner fabric of who they were. In his calm and serene way, and as only the Master of the universe could do, Jesus addressed the major issues of both their day and our twenty-first century. The essence of his message was, "It is time to let some things go!"

This is a message that cannot be avoided; we have to make a decision today and start out on a path that is quite different from the one on which we have been traveling. The Master of Galilee is telling us that the life we are living is destructive and is keeping us from the life God has for us. We are worried, stressed out, worn down, and downright burdened. Our mind is the battleground, and our bodies bear the scars. It is time to make a different move.

Both the first century and the twenty-first century demand a change. God's promise to us as we position ourselves for this new life is that, through him, a change is possible!

Jesus' opening words in Matthew 6:25–34 are, "Do not worry." The popular song by Bobby McFerrin comes to mind: "Don't worry, be happy." However, the Master does not say, "Don't worry, be happy." Jesus just says, "Do not worry." His reasoning is clear: Worrying will not produce happiness; it will, in fact, be a deterrent to it. He knows that we cannot tell ourselves to stop worrying; he also knows that with the help of God, we can, so he gives us encouragement that God is there with us in this tremendous act of faith. He assures us with this reminder:

- Look at nature. It survives and thrives without the fretful concerns of people.

- Look at the value of worrying. It does not change one thing.
- Look at your relationship to God, and know that he cares for you.

Jesus invites us back to our faith position. The beauty of faith is that it causes us to rethink our positions and our priorities. Jesus invites us to look at life through the eyes of our beliefs, not through the stressors that are attacking us. He is telling us that we have to let some things go, and we *will* be able to let them go by the power of God. What we are looking for, only God can provide.

## PITFALLS OF THE TWENTY-FIRST CENTURY

Whenever we are beset by the stresses or pitfalls of life, they are never isolated. They do not happen in a vacuum. They do not occur in a void. The problems in one room of our lives spill over into other rooms. They wind up affecting much of what we do and what we say. We are not so sophisticated that we can operate for long periods of time without there being some form of meltdown. We can muster up willpower, but only for so long. Like the cheetah of the African plains, we can run full speed for a time, and then our energy quickly dissipates. Our discontent begins to affect other areas of our lives.

There are links between our miseries and our predicaments. Problems in one area seem to make the climate ripe for problems in other areas. We may have a problem on the job, but if we are not able to let that problem go and move on, it will travel with us in the car, enter our living room when we arrive home, and begin to make its presence felt by all who come in contact with us. Issues from the past can corrupt the pleasantries of the present. Mistakes made yesterday can cloud opportunities waiting to burst forth today.

It may be a weight problem. We may be battling against the creeping advance of weight and its visible henchman, fat. Our attempts at dieting may not have been successful, and the stress of the weight is seen in the way we dress and the people and places we seek to avoid. It has a way of affecting our self-esteem and negatively working on our ability to see the purpose and productivity in ourselves.

Everything is interrelated. In order to get the esteem back, we have to work on the *real* problem. The real problem is not the weight, it is our obsession with weight. The real problem is not what it appears to be. The real problem is our emotional attachment with what we want to see happen and our endless quest to bring it to pass. Our dreams are not wrong; our hopes are not false. But a belief that we can muscle our way to happiness is an error. Such thinking causes families to fall apart, homes to break up, friendships to end, and children to be left at the gate.

For instance, some years ago, a friend of mine became embroiled in a battle on his job. The struggle began to consume his every waking thought. Each time he came over to our home, he talked about the people and what they had done to him and what they were still doing to him. It did not matter that we had also invited other guests who knew nothing of his plight. He would monopolize the conversation with the anger he held for his superiors. His marriage suffered, his relationships with his friends suffered, and his whole demeanor took on the look of his inner turmoil. He became consumed with what had happened at the workplace, and the problem began to spill over into the otherwise peaceful areas of his life.

Psychologists speak of psychosomatic illness, which is the physical manifestation of mind and body battles. The mind has not been able to let go and the body has picked up the struggle.

- Instead of an abundant life, we have an anxious life.
- Instead of a constructive life, we have a chaotic life.
- Instead of a fulfilled life, we have a fretful life.
- Instead of a whole life, we have holes in our life.

The Master says that this is not the plan or the way to live. Our lives are like ecosystems—problems in one portion of the system affect all the others. Pollutants put into the water upstream kill the fish downstream. That is why Jesus says that we must make a change. We are altering portions of our lives that we never intended to affect. Jesus says, "Let it go!" It is not worth what it does to our lives.

## ADVENT OF THE TWENTY-FIRST CENTURY

Let it go. This is a hard word for our self-sufficient age, but we see that it is nonetheless true. There are some things that we have to let God do for us. There are some things that we have to commit to heaven and trust God to take care of for us. The peace we are seeking is not in our power to attain. We need help; we need divine assistance. The happiness we seek through accomplishments can only come through our relationship with God. St. Augustine, the black bishop of Hippo, wrote, "My soul is not rested until it finds rest in thee." We seek the wrong prize. The Master asked an important question, "What does it profit us to gain the whole world and lose our souls?" *(Matthew 16:26, paraphrased)*. The soul is the real place of our dwelling. The actual seat of our happiness and pleasure is in the heart, not in the things we are seeking to acquire. It is in the interior of our being that we find happiness and wholeness. Perhaps that is why Jesus never cluttered his life with the quest for things. He gave himself ample space to develop his relationship with the only one who could and would make the soul leap and shout—God. Jesus specialized in inquiring, not in acquiring.

Happiness and wholeness can only be found in God. He alone has the prescription for our lives. He knows what we need, and he can overcome circumstances and situations to make it happen. Therefore, Jesus says in Matthew 6, "Don't worry. These things are in your heavenly Father's hands." The late Dr. T. Robert Washington, pastor of the Second Baptist Church in Philadelphia, was asked about a particular situation and whether he was worried about it. His reply was, "There is no reason for both God and me to worry about it. I cannot fix it, but he can." When all is said and done, it is what God does that really matters.

The Master is aware of how difficult it is for us to just let go. That is why, in Matthew 6:33 he tells us to replace our worry with wonder. As we navigate our way through the twenty-first century, Jesus exhorts us, "Seek first his kingdom and his righteousness, and all these things will be given to you as well" *(NIV)*. In order to let go, we have to take on. We let go of worry and take on wonder.

When we seek God's kingdom and the things of God, a change begins to take place within us. We become enthralled with the new quest and leave our burdens behind. This is what it means to be born again. We are born into a new kingdom with new realities, new excitements, and new wonders. Our position at work is important, but there is something more important. Our friends are nice, but our fellowship with God is unsurpassed.

Someone may ask, "But how do I seek God?" The answer is, one step at a time. First we must want to start by taking the first step. Look at the world, our life, and all that is about us and realize that someone bigger must be working behind the scenes. Look to Jesus. His kingdom is not only wonderful, it is full of wonder. There is so much that he wants to reveal to us. He will show us beauty that we have missed. He will give us back the smile that we thought we had forgotten. He will touch our hearts and play the strings of our souls with graceful skill. He will reach into our pain and massage away our misery. He will fill our minds with sights too wondrous to describe.

Real living does not begin until we seek his kingdom. It is in his kingdom that we will spend eternity; we need to become acquainted with it now. Jesus came to introduce this kingdom to us and show us how a kingdom citizen handles the stress and pressures of life. He came to show us how a kingdom citizen can "let it go." He can tell us because he walked this earth and lived through it. What we are looking for is not found in stress but in the Savior. Jesus alone is the answer, and only by residing in his kingdom can we truly let it go.

# 6

# HOLD ON!

How long, O Lord? Will you forget me forever? How long will you hide your face from me? How long must I wrestle with my thoughts and every day have sorrow in my heart? How long will my enemy triumph over me? Look on me and answer, O Lord my God. Give light to my eyes, or I will sleep in death; my enemy will say, "I have overcome him," and my foes will rejoice when I fall.But I trust in your unfailing love; my heart rejoices in your salvation.I will sing to the Lord, for he has been good to me.

*—Psalm 13, NIV*

## PROMISE OF THE TWENTY-FIRST CENTURY

FEW PEOPLE IN AMERICA have had the level of impact on modern life and society as the Rev. Dr. Martin Luther King Jr. His messages of hope and challenge forced our nation to recognize inequities and abolish barriers to people of color. In reading his life's story, one cannot help but be in awe of this prince of prophets.

One of the most powerful messages that Dr. King delivered was not heard from some great pulpit or some imposing platform. One of the messages most quoted and definitively associated with his ministry is a letter that he penned while languishing in a jail cell in Birmingham, Alabama, during the turmoil of the American civil rights movement and in an effort to win rights for the people of that city. We know it as "The Letter from the Birmingham Jail." In it, Dr. King laid out his belief in the rightness of his effort and put forth a challenge to people of good will to join him in this effort. He offered no apology for his actions but offered his detractors an invitation to be co-laborers in suffering and redemption. This letter is studied and dissected in seminaries and philosophy classes around the world. It is read and rehearsed as part of the King legacy. This epistle represents the pain of a man who knew there was much to do while realizing that there were few who were willing to put themselves on the line for the fundamental truth that "all people are created equal." One cannot read his words without feeling the pathos and pain that caused him to answer his critics and detractors with words such as these: "... One day the South will know that when these disinherited children of God sat down at lunch counters, they were in reality standing up for what is best in the American dream and for the most sacred values in our Judeo-Christian heritage, thereby bringing our nation back to those wells of democracy...." "One day," King wrote. Implicit in those two words is the admonition, "If we hold on."

For days, Dr. King feverishly wrote on whatever pieces of paper he could get his hands on. Finally, when the letter was finished, pieced together, and typed, it was twenty pages long. It was addressed to eight persons, but copies were distributed to the press and to others. What is interesting about this is the fact that the press paid no attention to it and the eight addressees did not even bother to respond. The letter in which King poured out his soul and stated clearly his rationale and credo went largely ignored. But the movement did not languish.

In the end, freedom was to belong not only to the African American citizens of Birmingham but to those across the country. A lesson lived and taught by the parents of those who came of age during the civil rights era was witnessed as true in that time of crisis for our country. This lesson declared, "He may not come when you want him, but he is always on time." He—Jesus—will be there; that is his promise to us. The challenge incumbent upon us is to stay strong until he does. Our faith must convince us, as it did Dr. King, to hold on against all odds!

Chapter 6

That promise that he will be there and the admonition to hold on are as true in this twenty-first century as they were in the previous century and centuries before the birth of Jesus. This is the message that the psalmist, King David, gives us in this concise, yet powerful, psalm. In the beginning of this psalm, we hear a cry from someone who is struggling with forces and factors that are determined to lay waste his life. We do not know what challenges rose up and invaded David's existence, sending his life into a tailspin, but we do know that the effort to keep going has been so exhausting that he is now *forced* to cry out. He can no longer keep his concerns to himself. He must be honest and open with God about how he feels and what disappointment he believes God has brought to his doorstep.

David not only needs help, but he *knows* that he needs help, and he is willing to call out for it. Most of us, at some point in our lives, will stand in the psalmist's shoes. As with David, there will have to be a "pouring out" from our hearts to Jesus before he can do a "pouring in" of his will in our lives. We must "humble (ourselves) before the Lord" *(James 4:10, NIV)*. This is the challenge that we face in the struggles of our mind, heart, and soul: Until we can get to that point of humility before God, the battles within us will keep on raging. Humility means that we must lay aside every weight, every false perception, every false pretense, every arrogant belief, and every defiant thought. We must submit ourselves to God on our knees, our heads bowed. We must strip, or be stripped, of the arrogance and pseudo strength that we have claimed and touted. Humility says, "When I need a shelter, when I need a friend, I go to the Rock." He will be there. Just hold on!

Looking again at Psalm 13, we see that David does not stop with his heart-emptying cry. The psalm does not end in despair or abandonment; rather it offers a new twist for those who have been twisted by life. It ends with the psalmist singing. David goes full circle. He starts out far from the land of music and ends on the mountain of rejoicing. How do we sing in the storm and make music in what is a miserable situation? The psalmist declares what Martin Luther

King Jr., manifested—we must be able to hold on!

King David lays out the path of despair to song in the middle of his plea. He says, "Look on me and answer, O Lord my God. Give light to my eyes, or I will sleep in death" *(Psalm 13:3, NIV)*. At this point, he is not looking for complete deliverance; he is looking for answers that will sustain him. The burden that he bears must be eased, and he is willing to accept just an answer for now. He does not need it all, nor does he want it all. He just wants to hear a word from God. Just a word. A word that can restore, encourage, strengthen, lift, promise, keep, abide, build, and fortify. In essence, he is crying out, "Just answer me. Speak a word. Say something to me, and I will be able to endure." That is all he needs for now, and he is willing to humble himself and ask for it.

Let this be an encouragement to anyone who sees nothing but the smoldering embers of a faded happiness and the onslaught of forces waiting to level the final blow. Hold on! After we have tasted the bitterest gall that life can dish out, God will complete his will in us. Listen to the words of the prophet Job: "... when he hath tried me, I shall come forth as gold" *(Job 23:10, KJV)*. Some may talk about how destroyed their lives are after some catastrophe, and that may be true, but it is not the end; there is life after the collapse. That is the very time when we must hold on!

As we chart our course in the twenty-first century, with all of the changes it is hoisting upon us, let us not discount this need. We will need to be able to stand when all around us is giving way. We will have to be strong when all around is faltering. We may feel abandoned. We may feel alone. There may be nothing but pain. There may be no light at the end of the tunnel. But listen to the last utterances of David in Psalm 13. He will not go down in defeat; he will not be a casualty on the battleground of his own experience. He will hold on: "But I trust in your unfailing love; my heart rejoices in your salvation. I will sing to the Lord, for he has been good to me" *(vv. 5–6, NIV)*.

Like David, we must hold on to the residue of our faith. God always comes to see about those who are making it on the residue.

The psalmist has doubts and fears, but in the end, he says, "I will trust," and "I will sing."

## PITFALLS OF THE TWENTY-FIRST CENTURY

Before King David's triumphal cry of trust and song, he fought battles on three fronts: his mind, his heart, and his flesh. He battled forces within and without. His mind, his thoughts, his reason, and his logic were all under attack. Make no mistake about it, mental attack can lay waste even the strongest of persons. It can cause the firmest legs to wobble. We do not know what came against the psalmist, but it took its toll on his ability to reason and think clearly.

His heart was also under attack. He could not find the proper emotions. His feelings lashed out at him, and he did not know what to think or feel. His soul was in turmoil. To add to these pressures, there was a physical situation that he could not resolve. His enemies had taken advantage of his vulnerability and were laying siege to him. They were, on more than one occasion, able to overwhelm his efforts and claim small victories. Here is someone who seems to be at the end of his rope.

Even today, whenever our mind and spirit are at variance with each other, the Adversary will cry, "Charge!" and bring chaos into the situation. In an era when we are used to placing the calls, pushing the buttons, and setting the agenda, we fall apart when things do not happen on our timetable. When we are suspended between events, it often feels as if we are prey caught in a spider's web. Our fear is that we will eventually be swallowed up by what we cannot control. Our anguish is caused by the fear that our fight is in vain and that our efforts will be placed in the file marked "insignificant." We cannot see an end to a long and tortuous path and therefore dismay at what appears to be one more step in futility.

The psalmist is not asking, "How much?" but rather, "How long?" He had seen enough to know that the issue was not how much trouble would come, because he knew that it would keep on coming. He also knew that regardless of how bad things were, they could always get worse. David was astute enough not to question quantity; his concern was duration. We need to understand and appreciate this plea of David. There will always be something coming in on us. Whether it is parents dismayed at the actions of their children or couples languishing in marriages that seem to be prisons for disappointment, we wrestle with how much we have to bear, when the real issue is "how long" do we have to bear it. What we need is the faith to hold on, the strength to see the situation through to the very end, and the patience to wait until we see the mighty hand of God at work.

## ADVENT OF THE TWENTY-FIRST CENTURY

Now, more than ever, there is a need for us to understand the power of patience. There has to be patience with the process and patience with the change. What God is trying to accomplish is going to take time. This twenty-first century finds us working out the details of a different social order, a more complex economic order, and a political order that defies categorization. All of these take time. We get anxious when things do not happen overnight, but it is not God's plan to do a "quick fix." It is his plan to create permanent, positive, and purposeful change. We have to accept that our lives are built on steps and that steps take longer than leaps. To be honest, much of our frustration comes because we cannot accept the reality that we must make cautious and careful strides into our future and toward our deliverance. We must learn that in some of the challenges of life, God calls us to take steps, not make leaps! Enough careful advances can help us cover the distance. In fact, the history of humanity is not a series of leaps. Our history is an account of baby steps, staggering steps, faltering steps, and sometimes giant steps. But it is a story of steps, nonetheless.

It was this kind of patience that enabled Moses to leave Egypt, go to Midian, and return to Egypt. It was patience that allowed Isaiah, Jeremiah, and Ezekiel to work with words for forty years, calling a nation to repentance. It was patience that forged a church from the cross of Calvary and made it a power of liberation for all time. We must accept the steps—and patience—that bring change into existence.

There is also a deeper truth that can strengthen us. All deliverance is not immediate. So often we want a deliverance that is inclusive and complete in its display, yet there are times when God does not pull us out of the pit. Instead, he gives us what we need to climb out of the pit ourselves! This is very different. Even David does not ask God to set him free. His burden is too great. He just wants some direction, some relief. Life can get so hectic that all we really want is relief. God knows that if the burden is shifted and rearranged just a little, we will develop the patience necessary to *hold on* until our deliverance comes.

We must also understand this: God will strengthen us even if he does not change the situation. The psalmist says, "My enemy will say, 'I have overcome him,' and my foes will rejoice when I fall" *(Psalm 13:4, NIV)*. Our enemies will gloat at the marriage that fails, the job that is lost, the child that is addicted to illegal drugs, the promotion that is denied, the scandal that is spread all over the newspapers. The enemies of the Kingdom take delight in any struggle faced by a child of God. How do we hold on when we know that the Enemy is waiting for our surrender? We hold on to the knowledge that our pain does not signal the end of the will of God in our lives. We may have to go through some terrible times, but this is not the end of the voyage. Even if we are made to look bad, the journey is not over, the gate is not closed. God does not want us to look bad, but he will allow the troubles and the pain to come if they accomplish a greater goal. And, rest assured, the greater goal brings us back the respect and the identity we long for and thought we had lost. We fear the failure, but God has a future for us. The moment may not go as we planned, and the defeat may be marked by the rejoicing of those who wanted us to slip, fall, or falter, but trust God. The story is not over; there is more to be written. There is a phoenix rising from the ruin and rubble of every broken dream and disappointment.

This is the simple yet powerful message of Easter. The omnipotence of God and the will of God were not defeated at the cross. Though mobs jeered and the powers of government and religion flexed mighty muscles as they led the Messiah to the tree, they did not hold all the cards. God allowed them their fifteen minutes of fame, their time of rejoicing, their fantasy of victory, but early on the third day, God completed his will and up from the grave came the resurrected Christ in all his splendor. Jesus was able to hold on through the agony of defeat on Friday. He believed in the will that sent him on his journey. In the end, God offered a greater victory than one that could have been achieved short of the grave.

As for King David at the end of Psalm 13, we are not told when his help arrived. Perhaps that is important. There is no timetable set for his release. We are left with the image of a man who will hold on as long as it takes. He offers us the road that he traveled and the strength it gave to him. David says, "I trust ... I will sing" *(vv. 5,6, NIV)*. Notice that trusting is an act of the will and singing is an act of the soul. Trusting speaks to the battle in his mind, singing speaks to the storm in his heart. He resolves to defeat the forces that attack him with the weapons of spiritual warfare: trust and song. He will lean on God and sing praises to his name. The trust will birth the song, and the song will strengthen the trust. They will go hand in hand together, and in the end, David will make it. This will encourage him all the days of his appointed time.

# 7

# REJOICE EVERMORE!

Finally, my brothers, rejoice in the Lord! It is no trouble for me to write the same things to you again, and it is a safeguard for you.... Rejoice in the Lord always. I will say it again: Rejoice!

—*Philippians 3:1; 4:4, NIV*

## PROMISE OF THE TWENTY-FIRST CENTURY

BEFORE THE COLLAPSE of the Soviet Union—of which Russia was the center—and the end of the Cold War era in United States-Russian relations, I was privileged to be part of a group visiting that country. We were there to observe and study the Christian revival that was taking place and to witness the first May Day celebration that was not tightly orchestrated by the government. Our journey was based in the capital of Moscow, the great city of the czars, the home of the famous Kremlin, and the burial place of Lenin. Too the concepts of *glasnost* and *perestroika* were revolutionizing the way the nation thought and acted.

Yet our excitement was tempered when we actually arrived in that majestic old city. We did not see the beauty that gripped Tolstoy or Dostoevsky. Modern Moscow, though housing the great symbols of Russian architecture such as St. Basil's Cathedral, looked bleak, gray, solemn, and sad. There was a heavy weight upon the city. Creativity had been exiled by previous regimes, and all the buildings looked alike. The architecture was boxy, no longer grand and glorious, and the structures looked bland. The people's faces seemed to reflect the outer circumstances of their lives. They looked old and tired. As we walked the sidewalks we noticed the blank looks on their faces. It was a disappointing sight to see.

Hearing their stories was, to say the least, even sadder and more heart wrenching. Yes, there was a new leader, the government had changed, and the official policy of the nation was boldly different, but their hope was struggling to exist. The condition of the economy, the civil uprisings in other Soviet states, and the failure of the new government policies to reverse the downward spiral of their monetary fortunes had them in such a quandary that they were cynical about their future, both individually and as a nation. There was but one word to describe their view of life—pessimistic.

That was the condition of Russia and its citizens as they neared the end of the twentieth century, but it also mirrors America as we put down roots in the twenty-first century. Our news media paint a sad picture of life. Front-page newspaper and newsmagazine articles and television news readers give us very little but the most horrible stories. This is not an indictment of the news media; they are openly reporting what has actually happened somewhere, some time, and we the consumers are clamoring for more of the unbelievable, the unfathomable, and the sensational. It is almost as if we have actually become what we see on television and read descriptions of in print. Drive-by shootings take hundreds of victims off our streets. Gangland activity has transformed the look and feel of too many of our neighborhoods. Crime and corruption raise their ugly heads in the most principled people and situations. There is a dark cloud that hangs over our lives. Viewers and readers can only turn to one another and ask, "Is there *anything* good happening anywhere in the world?"

The answer to this question is a resounding, "Yes!" There is a way to squash this fatalistic, pessimistic outlook. There is a way to see good when evil seems to have the upper hand. From millennium to millennium, the world has kept on spinning. Life has unfolded, generations have emerged. We have to take stock of our lives and the history of our world and realize this promise: The

Lord did not bring us this far to leave us now! When we look carefully at who Christ is and what calling him Lord means to us, we will recognize that he has made a difference in our lives and in our place on this earth every day of our existence. Moreover, because of him, nothing is as bad as it could be, and everything is better than we deserve.

This knowledge of who God is makes us change our focus from earth to heaven. Remembering the *omnipotent* nature of God takes us beyond our human situation and puts us squarely at the throne of God. Recognizing the *omniscient* nature of God reverses the way we see life and declares that there is another approach. In the heat of our anxieties and gloom, recalling the *omnipresent* nature of God lets us stand firmly on the knowledge that the Lord will be there for us. Inherent in his nature is the promise that he will not forsake us in any way, any time!

## PITFALLS OF THE TWENTY-FIRST CENTURY

Still, even with the knowledge that we have such a mighty God and Savior in our midst, we have become almost obsessed with the negative. We often conclude that the dubious outcome is destined to be ours. We have lost our hope and are on the verge of surrendering our faith. Too many of us have already determined that no remedy will alleviate our despair. It is as if we are hopelessly adrift on the sea of life, and we have successfully convinced ourselves that no rescue effort has been or ever will be launched.

This pitfall of the twenty-first century should not be viewed as a condition that is confined to modern times; it has been experienced throughout the ages. Two thousand years ago, the apostle Paul recognized this classic symptom of human frailty when he addressed the saints in Philippi. The Philippian believers had every reason to be pessimistic. The Romans were ruling, and they were a struggling Christian community in the heartland of Caesar worship. They were being persecuted daily; their confession of faith was being distorted. Their ability to freely express their faith was being undermined. They had little to see as positive. To add insult to injury, the Judaizers were trying to enforce their kind of Christianity on this fledgling community, and two women in the group—Euodia and Syntyche—were locked in an openly contentious dispute. The church was battling both internal and external pressures. The tiny church was struggling with issues that, along with the other forces the people were facing, was enough to cause them great despair.

Paul's plight was far greater than theirs. Yes, the Philippian Christians were subject to the Romans, but Paul was under their arrest. His life was soon to end. The future for him was a matter of months, weeks, and days. "The time of his departure was at hand." The Lord had called Paul into this work, and his end was to be the same as the Master's. What hope could he give if this was so? What word other than a pessimistic one could fall from his lips? What could transform his thinking from bitterness to blessedness?

The tent maker was facing death, but he was not discouraged. "I desire to depart and be with Christ, which is better by far; but it is more necessary for you that I remain in the body" *(Philippians 1:23–24, NIV)*. Paul was going to face what he had to face, and he was going to confront it with a shout, not a sigh. He was not going to spend his last days in sadness with a disheartened spirit. Neither was he going to look with desperation at the state of humanity. Paul rose to the occasion. He knew that when we have been overwhelmed and saturated with problems, it is time to look at them in a different way. He also understood the words of the psalmist:

"I will lift up mine eyes unto the hills ..." *(Psalm 121:1, KJV)*.

"I will bless the Lord at all times: his praise shall continually be in my mouth" *(Psalm 34:1, KJV)*.

Paul took these few words of Scripture and created a sound bite of hope and encouragement. The power and impact of this message upon the human race have rarely been equaled. He said to the people of Philippi, "Rejoice in the Lord always. I will say it again: Rejoice!" *(Philippians 4:4, NIV).*

## ADVENT OF THE TWENTY-FIRST CENTURY

Notice the formula presented by Paul. He says, "Rejoice *in the Lord* always." Our rejoicing is grounded in the Lord. Our rejoicing is based on the Lord God. Our rejoicing is attached to our God. Paul is essentially saying, "Keep your praise and your faith, your shout and your song, your hope and your happiness grounded in the power of knowing that the Lord is your God."

When circumstances and situations grip our lives, something must come along to unlock the vault and let the rejoicing come forth. When we sing, "When I think of the goodness of Jesus and all he's done for me, my soul cries out hallelujah, thank God for saving me," we are in essence causing the hinges to be torn from the vault. When we think about the meaning of Christ in our lives and how he

- saves us
- heals us
- delivers us
- protects us
- lifts us
- blesses us
- dries our tears
- calms our fears
- keeps our hope

when we consider his contribution to our lives, we cannot help but rejoice. Moreover, if the moment is seemingly unbearable, our meditation on his place in our lives has a way of empowering us to overcome even the worst of moments. This is where we go for relief from the burden of living in such a pessimistic age.

Our rejoicing is in the fact that there is a God who rules above. It is rejoicing in the knowledge that he is *our* God and will be our guide. It is rejoicing in the understanding that in every situation he gives consolation. It is the sound of a soul that knows it will survive the pressure. It is the sound of one who has found something more important than plight and pain to concentrate on. It has the sound of one who prefers the vision of the Kingdom to the groans of the space we inhabit on this earth. It is the sound of one who can challenge the forces of this world because they have gained strength for the battle by praising the Lord. " ... In thy presence is fulness of joy; at thy right hand are pleasures for evermore" *(Psalm 16:11, KJV)*.

To be sure, Paul says that our rejoicing is to be in the Lord, but he also says that we are to rejoice always. Our weapon against the morass of the age is not intermittent rejoicing, but rejoicing that breaks out at any time and in any place.

It is the absence of rejoicing that gives the Enemy an opportunity to enter our minds and our spirits and contaminate them with despair that floods our lives. Rejoicing serves to keep our souls guarded. It is the boundary that keeps the Enemy out. If the sword of the Spirit is our weapon against the Adversary when we are engaged in battle, then rejoicing is the sentinel that watches the camp and sounds the alarm at the approach of the Enemy.

Since we do not always know what is lurking about in our souls, waiting for an opportunity to penetrate our defenses and sneak in where our shields are down, every now and then we must clear the area of intruders. We can go into a rejoicing mode and watch the Enemy flee! As we rejoice, the spiritual temperature around our life rises to a point where *evil must move out*:

- When we rejoice in our car on the way to work, our day's workload does not seem so tedious.
- When we rejoice as we enter our homes, forces of evil cannot follow us through the door.
- As we rejoice in the heat of an argument, statements that are best left unsaid are never uttered.

It is our rejoicing over who God is and who he is to us that causes the Adversary to realize he will not succeed in his attack. "Our minds are kept in perfect peace" because we trust in the Lord. He steps in and, with a blast of his presence, clears our souls of any corruption. Jesus purifies the space both around us and within us.

Once we start to rejoice and enjoy the pure pleasure of the Spirit of the Lord alive and well within us, we cannot stop the praise, even when we feel we want to. We begin to feel how it is possible to follow Paul's directive to rejoice in the Lord always. There may be times when we want to regain our composure, but we cannot stop our worship unless *he* lets us go. This must have been what Jesus meant when he responded to the Pharisees on the road to Jerusalem. Jesus was on his way to the city, seated on the back of a donkey. The crowd was cheering and shouting praises to his name. The Pharisees asked Jesus to stop the uproar, but he responded, "… If these should hold their peace, the stones would immediately cry out" *(Luke 19:40, KJV).* What really happened was that the Master looked at the crowd and realized it was too late. Once the crowd began their hosannas, there was no stopping them. If the people did stop before their time, the shouts that were left unfinished would spill over into the rocks.

That is real rejoicing! The result of such joy is victory over the oppressive forces and situations we face as we enter into the abundant life. Seek both to live victoriously *and* abundantly. This is the blessing we get from rejoicing. The primal purpose is recreated. Once again, we are back to where we were created to be. We are where Adam and Eve were before the Fall. We are where Jesus was after the resurrection. Rejoicing lets us know that God not only loves the world, he loves us, too. He loves us with all our mistakes, all our baggage, and all our needs. He takes each one of these burdens and ministers to us. When he finishes, we cannot explain what has happened; all we know is that because of him the space we thought was cluttered with debris and rubble has been cleared. We stumble about, looking for the trash to still be there, but it is gone. All that lingers is the memory of his presence in our hearts. There is but one thing for us to do at that point—rejoice again. Praise him!

"Praise God from whom all blessings flow. Praise him all creatures here below. Praise him above, ye heavenly host. Praise Father, Son, and Holy Ghost."

# 8

# NO WEAPON SHALL PROSPER

"If anyone does attack you, it will not be my doing; whoever attacks you will surrender to you. See, it is I who created the blacksmith who fans the coals into flame and forges a weapon fit for its work. And it is I who have created the destroyer to work havoc; no weapon forged against you will prevail, and you will refute every tongue that accuses you. This is the heritage of the servants of the Lord, and this is their vindication from me," declares the Lord.

*—Isaiah 54:15-17, NIV*

## PROMISE OF THE TWENTY-FIRST CENTURY

SOME YEARS AGO, a preacher recounted the following story in the opening comments of his sermon. During the Battle of Britain, when Hitler's air armada tried to cripple and crush the last great stronghold of European freedom, Sir Winston Churchill received a note of encouragement from Bermuda, one of the British colonies. The note simply read, "Fight on Britain, Bermuda is behind you." With the full weight of the German air force dropping bomb after bomb upon the city, the note was encouraging, but it was also clear that if the British wavered, the tiny island of Bermuda, nestled in the waters of the Atlantic Ocean and closer to the United States than to Britain, would be of little help. They had made a gallant proclamation, but it was obvious they did not have what was needed to back it up.

Promises are only as good as the people who make them. They

do not have power in and of themselves to effect their own guarantee; they rely solely on the good faith and resources of the one making the claim. Many of us have learned this lesson the hard way. From childhood through our adult years, we live our lives believing that someone's word is their bond. We even teach our children, "Don't make promises you don't plan to keep." Yet people have made promises to us that they could not keep. They have pledged what they did not provide. They have extracted but not extended. They have said one thing and done another.

We need not look any further than the history of our own nation to find concrete examples. African American people were promised forty acres and a mule, but have yet to see either the land or the animal. Our forefathers were promised but not provided. The indigenous American people—Native Americans—were promised land and resources. Instead, they were herded onto reservations and brought to the point of the near extinction of their culture. They were given the word of the nation, but political expediency canceled the promise.

The strength of a promise is in the character and the content of the one who makes it. Whether individually or as a nation, all we have is our word. Without it, we are not better than the rabble and ruffians who lie at the drop of a hat. It was laudable for Bermuda to send the telegram, but if the German juggernaut had succeeded in destroying Britain's Royal Air Force, Bermuda would have been of little or no help. The British needed someone who could back up the pledge.

The truth of the matter is that we also need someone who can back up what is promised and can guarantee what is proposed. We need to know that the rug will not be pulled from under us and whatever was pledged will come to pass. We want assurances that our blessings are not at the mercy of others and will not be snatched from us. We also want to feel confident that the efforts of our enemies will not succeed. We want to be sure that the enemies within and without are not going to be victorious. We need someone who can support words with power and decisions with strength. We want to be sure that we are not depending on Bermuda!

There *is* someone who can make such a claim. When his word has gone forth, it is as much as done. He says what he means and means what he says. Moreover, he stands behind *everything* he says. There is one who can uphold every word with deeds; he can make things happen when he declares they will come to pass. That someone is none other than the one we know as Jehovah, the Lord God Almighty. He keeps his word.

This is a word for all who see God leading them down a new road in this twenty-first century when the past road has been littered with missteps, regrets, and mistakes. This promise is for

- the weary,
- the fragile,
- the frightened,
- the alarmed,
- the hurting,
- the shamed,
- the fallen, and
- the failure.

This is the word for the prodigal who has returned home, the sinner who has confessed his or her sins, and the person who has just said yes to God after a long period of saying no. To these people the Lord makes this promise: "If anyone does attack you … no weapon forged against you will prevail *(Isaiah 54:15,17, NIV)*. This is a message for us all when we decide to go forward boldly by following a new vision or confronting a formidable obstacle. The Lord stands behind his word; we will not be held back. "No weapon that is formed against thee shall prosper!" *(Isaiah 54:17, KJV)*.

## PITFALLS OF THE TWENTY-FIRST CENTURY

The prophet Isaiah made this claim to a people who had lost their hope. The people of Israel had returned to the land of their birth with the memory that it was once a place they called home. They remembered that it was their sins that caused them to lose the place they loved and their indiscretions that had mounted up to heaven. They were subject to another nation, having been taken by force from their homes and driven into captivity. They lost their dreams and their hopes. Standing outside their place of fellowship, they wondered if this was just a brief hiatus before they would be returned to yet another captivity. Surveying their homeland, they realized just how tenuous their position really was. They understood that it could all be taken away in the twinkling of an eye. They were fearful that they would, once again, be sent packing for points and parts unknown.

Most of us in our more honest moments would have to admit that our lives—several millennia after the people of Israel first returned to their homeland—are still held together by forces we do not completely understand. How we manage to keep everything intact often astounds us. We could lose it all so quickly. One week of unemployment would send us crashing into economic ruin. We may have a good job and a good position, but we can come tumbling down from that perch very easily. The truth is that the older we get and the more responsibilities we have, the more this burden weighs upon our spirits and causes us to be seriously concerned about issues of security and stability. We cannot afford to have the weapons prosper that are formed against us.

Even when we decide to take new steps in the right direction, circumstances may rise up against us that cause us to question whether there is any hope for change. We think that God is punishing us for things we have done wrong. Yet the Lord wants us to realize that the troubles that arise when we are in a state of newness and freshness are not sent by him. "If anyone does attack you, it will not be my doing ..." *(Isaiah 54:15, NIV).*

When we are in a fragile state, we have to understand that the attacks that come are not part of some divine punishment. They are the contracted work of the Adversary; he is the one behind the new attack. What we are facing is not from God, but the rumblings of a beggar about to lose his cup. Satan has been expelled and is trying to hold on. He has formed weapons to keep us in bondage. He wants us physically, mentally, emotionally, and spiritually chained and bound to the darkness of a dying kingdom.

Every time we say no to the plan of evil and to the kingdom of wickedness and decidedly move toward our God, a part of Satan's kingdom of darkness dies. It is laid waste. Its residents—envy, strife, contention, confusion, duplicity, hypocrisy—are all forced to move and find a new residence. This becomes the pronouncement from the Lord: "… whoever attacks you will surrender to you" *(Isaiah 54:15, NIV)*. The Enemy cannot win. In fact, the Word does not say they will just be defeated; it declares that they will raise the flag of surrender and place their weapons in your hands. All of them will surrender: the lies, the hate, the deception, the confusion, the depression, the frustration, and the pain. They will not just run away; they will stand as you enter as conqueror. They will be forced to declare, "Greater is he that is in you than he that is in the world!"

We may be fragile and culpable, like a baby chick breaking out of its eggshell, but trust the promise. The light will not fail us, and the victory will be ours.

## ADVENT OF THE TWENTY-FIRST CENTURY

Isaiah 54 opens with a major word for the returning people. The Lord comes to the scene with a charge that is both refreshing and reaffirming. The chapter opens with a call for the people to think big and expand their vision! God tells them to get out of the narrow thinking that has governed them since their release and look forward to a new day with greater opportunities and challenges. No, they have not been all that they should be. Their sins have been grievous, but all that is behind them now. The Lord their God has forgiven them and has destined and determined a new life for them.

Humanity can be so unforgiving and unyielding in its pronouncements, but God, the author and the finisher of life—the one responsible for all that we have and ever hope to be—is willing and able to forgive us and give us a second chance. The people of Israel should have returned as hirelings, but instead God blessed them and told them to enlarge their tents! They were given another chance and then told:

> "Do not be afraid; you will not suffer shame.
> Do not fear disgrace; you will not be humiliated.
> You will forget the shame of your youth
> and remember no more the reproach
> of your widowhood" *(Isaiah 54:4, NIV).*

This is a word of restoration and hope. The Lord did not plan for the rug to be pulled from under them. Their efforts would not crash upon the rocks. The Lord made a promise to the weary and the fragile: They would not journey to the end of the rainbow only to be disappointed.

The Lord then added a second level of assurance for the people. They were not in the fight alone. God has accepted his role in our struggle. He says through the prophet, "See, it is I who created the blacksmith who fans the coals into flame and forges a weapon fit for its work. And it is I who have created the destroyer to work havoc" *(Isaiah 54:16, NIV).*

Regardless of what tries to bring us down or wound the progress of our faith, it will be stymied and stopped by the Lord, because he is the one who has total control. He says, "The blacksmith that makes the weapon was created by me!" He knows the ins and outs of everything that is posed against us; he can bring their efforts to naught. This is one of the most refreshing realizations for those of us who have weary moments. God says it will not be up to us to produce the victory. He promises to undergird the work so that it will not fail. He has not brought us this far to let the Evil One take us back. He will provide resources of every kind to insure our victory. He will make himself a part of the battle. He will speak to us in the car, through the radio, in conversation, through billboards, in books, at movies … anywhere we are, he will be there speaking a word of power and purpose to us. He will even step in to build a barrier between us and the Adversary. The Evil One will exhaust his energy while we outlast the storm.

That is why, when we feel as if we are about to give up, a new surge of power comes upon us and we are able to stand. That is God working on our behalf. He is not going to let us go down in defeat. He knows his role in our struggle. We need his gentle touch. We need his encouraging word. We need his powerful hand. We need his visible signs. God does not mind giving us all these things.

The Lord ends his word to the weary with a universal commitment that "No weapon formed against you will prevail" *(Isaiah 54:17, NIV)*. It does not matter what comes against us. He will defend us and bring evil to naught. This means that we can replace our fears with faith. We can venture forward into the unknown realms of the millennium knowing that we will stand and survive. God is going to get us where we need to be. We cannot get ourselves there, but his promise keeps us going and makes us confident of this: "… the sufferings of this present time are not worthy to be compared with the glory which shall be revealed in us" *(Romans 8:18, KJV)*.

Even Jesus accepted the word of the prophet that no weapon against him would prosper. Every weapon known by the world of his day was turned on him, from the inner indignity and humiliation of a questionable birth to the shame of his ignominious death on the cross. Friends and family joined with foes to decry his actions and activities. He was wounded and bruised, but he kept on going.

Some might say, "Then explain Calvary. I thought no weapon would prosper?" Well, look at Calvary. Evil planned not to just kill Jesus but to kill the movement of freedom and liberation. The plan was to stop the Kingdom of God and hold forever captive the people of the promise. Yet this plan did not prosper. The Enemy killed Jesus' body, but in doing so, he released into the world a far greater presence—the Holy Spirit. He is living in our hearts right now.

- Did it prosper? There is a church on every corner.
- Did it prosper? Believers are called by his name.
- Did it prosper? Healing and deliverance take place.
- Did it prosper? We are saved.
- Did it prosper? Our children are made whole.
- Did it prosper? Victory is ours.
- Did it prosper? The kingdom of God has truly come!

# 9

# INQUIRING MINDS WANT TO KNOW

Three days later he called together the leaders of the Jews.
When they had assembled, Paul said to them: "My brothers,
although I have done nothing against our people or against
the customs of our ancestors, I was arrested in Jerusalem and
handed over to the Romans. They examined me and wanted
to release me, because I was not guilty of any crime deserving
death. But when the Jews objected, I was compelled to appeal
to Caesar—not that I had any charge to bring against my own
people. For this reason I have asked to see you and talk with
you. It is because of the hope of Israel that I am bound with
this chain." They replied, "We have not received any letters
from Judea concerning you, and none of the brothers who have
come from there has reported or said anything bad about you.
But we want to hear what your views are, for we know that
people everywhere are talking against this sect." They arranged
to meet Paul on a certain day, and came in even larger numbers
to the place where he was staying. From morning till evening
he explained and declared to them the kingdom of God and
tried to convince them about Jesus from the Law of Moses
and from the Prophets. Some were convinced by what he said,
but others would not believe.

*—Acts 28:17-24, NIV*

# Chapter 9

## PROMISE OF THE TWENTY-FIRST CENTURY

THE PREVAILING VIEW of our time is that people are not really serious or interested in matters of faith or religion. This age resembles a selfish generation, concerned only about the triumvirate "me, myself, and I." If we look only on the outside of our culture we could very easily conclude that there is little interest in God. We have watched the transition of our society from a southern, rural, religious culture to an urban, humanistic, and self-serving culture. We have watched Easter move from a Sunday of religious celebration marked by new suits and dresses for church to a Sunday that is a part of any other weekend and recognizable by sweat suits and a jog around the neighborhood. The music on the airwaves and the messages emanating from television, videos, books, magazines, and newspapers seem to betray an almost morbid sense of life where nihilism and fatalism have replaced Christian theism.

However, many of us have been taught never to judge a book by its cover; that adage is still true concerning matters of faith and religion. The problem is not that people are disinterested in the things of God; there is something in each and every one of us that cries out to know about the one who created us and put us in this place:

- Families holding dead bodies that were murdered in drive-by shootings is a cry for answers.
- Young people shooting classmates in Columbine, Colorado, is a cry for answers.
- People flocking to bookstores to purchase the latest secular "self-help" book is a cry for answers.

Life has taken its toll on humanity. The pain and agony, the confusion and chaos, and the hope and dream of a better life have caused even the hardest of souls to cry out for some kind of clarification. People *do* want to know if there is a word from God! The problem is that few people can adequately articulate the questions they have about God. In days past, cries for answers about God could be understood clearly. But in this day of hip hop, heavy metal, ebonics, and the drug and crime culture, language patterns have changed, our speech has become garbled, and we cannot understand the cry. Not only that, it has become increasingly difficult to find people who can provide answers and whose lives and witness are consistent with those answers!

Some time ago *The National Enquirer* used as its advertising slogan the phrase, "Inquiring Minds Want to Know." They sold countless issues because their premise was correct; people really did want to know the kinds of sensational news that was printed on their pages. In the same way, inquiring minds in the twenty-first century want to know. There is a great hunger and a burning need for people to really understand themselves. They instinctively sense that the answers will not be gleaned from the hottest video, the steamiest novel, or the most explicit song lyrics. The answers will not be found in the latest fashion craze, the most recently updated automobile design, or the trendiest neighborhood.

This is where Jesus steps in. He keeps the promise that he made thousands of years ago in Deuteronomy 31:8 *(NIV)* and that he is still keeping today: "… he will never leave you nor forsake you…." In the midst of society's groping and groaning and futile knocking at every door but that of the Kingdom, Jesus will not forsake us. He knows that we just want to understand the archetype of human personality, the Lord Jesus Christ. He knows that seekers want to know how he has infused his person and personality into the lives of those who are his. Even though more people pass by churches than venture to enter through their doors, it is not lost on him that humanity is still curious about the mystique surrounding the church and the people of God. He knows that people intuitively realize this is not a gimmick or a game. They still want to know what it is that believers have found, and they want that same something to be a part of their lives. They desire to become one of his followers.

Because he has promised never to forsake us, he lets us keep seeking until we hear and accept the only answer. He makes us aware of an inward journey that has outward consequences. If we are to survive the rigorous pulls and tugs of this new era, we must return to the desire to know ourselves at the deepest levels, the levels where

Chapter 9

God dwells. Whether in this millennium, two thousand years ago in the time of the apostle Paul, or in some other past age, inquiring minds want to know, and God still provides the answers.

## PITFALLS OF THE TWENTY-FIRST CENTURY

During the time of Jesus there was a Pharisee in Jerusalem named Nicodemus, a member of the Jewish ruling council. He was steeped in the tradition of his people, yet he had seen the impotence of his people and their faith. The religion had degenerated to a remnant of quotes and practices, while the fire of faith seemed lost to dead prophets and long-gone sages. The religion had no power, and the people had no hope. Something was missing. Nicodemus knew that God was not the problem; the problem was that God's people no longer knew how to connect to him. They knew the words of the Scriptures, but they had lost the God of the Scriptures.

Nicodemus had heard the teachings of Jesus and seen the miraculous signs he was performing. He wanted to know more and understand more about this "teacher from God." There is an interesting aspect to this story. Nicodemus came by night to see Jesus. He did not come openly to Jesus for fear of the people who affirmed his status as a leader among the Jews. He was not willing to just come out in the open. However, we cannot forget that he still wanted a revelation. He came at night, but he did come. Nicodemus came to Jesus to ask questions. The dialogue that follows is well known by many of us. Nicodemus affirmed what he believed about Jesus and then the Master uttered the words, "… no one can see the kingdom of God unless he is born again" *(John 3:3, NIV)*. Those words say it all.

Like Jesus, we need to know how to interpret the questions of the Nicodemuses—the seekers—of this age and how to answer them with clarity and direction. There are many who have sensed the emptiness of that which they call god, and they are witnessing a new vitality breaking out all around them. When we look beyond economics and social standing and hear the cry of the heart, what we actually hear is the cry of every heart. There are professionals and police officers, philosophers and plumbers, politicians and dieticians who are beginning to recognize that a new power is emerging all around and that there are those who seem to be blessed by its presence. There are so many who want to be liberated from the dark forces of life, and they are the ones who look to us—believers and the church community—and look at us with inquiring minds and hearts.

Yet we seem to be slipping in our ability to recognize and speak to this wider, seeking community. This is one of the major pitfalls or challenges of the twenty-first century. We have focused on persons who speak a certain way and think a certain way, but we have missed the transformation that has taken place in our culture and society. We are not keeping abreast of the changes. Not everyone is ready, willing, or able to walk out into the light to see Jesus. Some are slipping in. Some come under the shade of night. They do not tell their friends they are coming. They try to sit where no one will notice them. They try to ignore conversations about their faith so that others will not know they believe. They come at night. They want to know, but they are afraid to tell the rest of their crew that the life they share with them is missing the mark.

We do not speak the language of those who will not seek answers in the light. There are teens who are tired of the struggle with their peers. There are adults who are tired of the dog-eat-dog workplace. There are people who are tired of the emptiness and the loneliness. These people want to see Jesus, and they will come to see Jesus, but they are coming by night. We, on the other hand, have missed the transformation that has taken place in our culture and society. Our world has radically changed, and we are not keeping abreast of the changes. We see this new type of "nighttime seeker" as an aberration that will eventually return to normal, but this is not true. Normal is being redefined, and the good old days are gone forever. Until we realize this, we will be ineffective in helping the Nicodemuses of our age understand the person and power of Jesus Christ and how he transforms lives.

Chapter 9

# ADVENT OF THE TWENTY-FIRST CENTURY

It is important to note that Nicodemus came to see *Jesus*. He wanted to be involved with the Master and dialogue with him. He did not come to be awed by the group of twelve disciples and the itinerary they kept. He wanted to get into the mind and head of the Master. He wanted to see and feel and touch the spirit of the man who gave him hope for himself.

It is important to take note of this because, in our witnessing efforts, we often forget what it is we are presenting. Too many of us are presenting our church and its organizational plan for fulfilling its ministry. We do not appreciate that it is the majesty of the personality of Jesus that causes Nicodemus and thousands of others to come forward. The key word is *personality*. That is what Paul meant when he said, "Let this mind be in you which was also in Christ Jesus" *(Philippians 2:5, KJV)*. His personality must be seen in us, and we must be so convinced of its presence and its power that we do not hide behind other things and make them substitutes for Christ. We present our church because we think it is a better representation of Christ than we are. We present our preacher because we think she or he is a better representation than we are. We present some other saint because we feel his or her walk and talk is better than our own. Yet it is our transformed life and the power that transformed us that must be presented. We are "the epistle of Christ … written not with ink, but with the Spirit of the living God; not in tables of stone, but in fleshy tables of the heart" *(2 Corinthians 3:3, KJV)*. The greatest sermon does not come from a pulpit but from a life. We are called to remember that inquiring minds want to understand the one who lives in us.

This means that we have work to do. We must take time to understand what the Lord has done and is doing in our lives. We must take time to understand who we were and who we are becoming. The power of the Lord is so revolutionary and transforming that we are not who we once were, and a new path has been opened to us. This new path assures us fellowship with all that is a part of heaven. Our salvation requires that we take time with God and become familiar with his ways and his thoughts. The prophet Isaiah stated the need for this centuries before Nicodemus came on the scene: "For my thoughts are not your thoughts, neither are your ways my ways, saith the Lord. For as the heavens are higher than the earth, so are my ways higher than your ways, and my thoughts than your thoughts" *(Isaiah 55:8–9, KJV)*.

It takes time to know God, to understand him, and above all to appreciate what he has done through the death of Jesus and what he is offering to the world. Once we realize this, our witness takes on new meaning. We have purpose, and that purpose is to present Christ. We have a mission—to draw the lost into his kingdom. We have a desire—to see others come into the saving knowledge of the Lord. This drive rises to the surface whenever some seeker asks questions about the power that seems so strong and real in our lives.

If every Christian understood this truth, we would be able to offer light where there is darkness and hope where there is despair. This is the need of the world and the cry of its people. God is calling on his church to speak power to chaos, but the church cannot accomplish this task if it has lost its ability to understand its own language. We can no longer spew out religious jargon and pious statements of faith. We must believe in the power of God as revealed in Jesus, and we must be able to manifest it in our lives. Our witness is the result of the fire in our heart that is explained through the words of our mouth. Our heart opens the door to others, and our words escort those individuals into the Master's presence. The language of faith is the language of the heart.

Look at the Master. His miracles were not calculated performances designed to win followers or increase congregational size. They were not ratings efforts in a world of major rabbis and teachers. He was, as the Scriptures say, "… moved with compassion …" *(Matthew 9:36, KJV)*. It was compassion that caused him to heal

- the mother-in-law of Peter,
- the man with the withered hand,
- the leper,

- the Syrophoenician woman,
- Lazarus,
- Jairus' daughter,
- the woman with the issue of blood, and a host of others.

He did it because his heart was touched and he had the power to make a difference. Perhaps our hearts are not touched because we do not believe we have the power to make a difference and we do not want to set ourselves up for disappointment. That might be our problem. Yet we must believe what we know in our minds and feel in our hearts. We must say no to that voice that seeks to make us doubt what we believe. If we are to help those in darkness, then we must believe that the power of God is real and that God has purposed to work through us. The writer of Hebrews 11:6 *(KJV)* says it best: "… he that cometh to God must believe that he is, and that he is a rewarder of them that diligently seek him." We have to believe, and when we do the compassion will come bursting forth from us. We will speak in winsome tones to people who are in the hotbed of disappointment and despair. Let the church start believing and the world will start receiving. That is what Jesus wanted from us all along. He wanted us to believe because, in our doing so, his church would be built and the rock upon which it would be constructed would be unmovable.

Inquiring minds want to know because they have seen what faith can do. It is our faith that people seek to understand, our faith that draws them out of the darkness. When they see what believing can produce in our lives, they realize that it is not some illusive idea but a principle that gives substance to our daily walk. Faith has opened doors, healed bodies, saved families, paid bills, and created opportunities. The church has a history with faith and the world has watched, sometimes in unbelief and at other times with sheer astonishment, how one person—or one group of people—believing in God could make such a difference.

The key to this story of Nicodemus is that he came with questions and with the hope of a life-changing encounter. This has been the reality ever since Adam and Eve lost their garden paradise.

There has always been a part of God in the world because he "did not leave himself without a witness" *(Acts 14:17, NASB)*. People have always seen glimmers of his power and glory and wondered how they, too, could be so blessed. Yet in Jesus, God showed it all and gave it all. In Jesus, God showed us who we could be and then offered us the opportunity to have it. All we have had to do is say yes. Then we have to be ready to transmit. That is the challenge. We must receive the news that is offered but stay ready to transmit that truth to others who are still on the path of the seeker. We cannot build our three booths and stay on the mountain. We must come back to the valley and realize that the blessing of the mountain is not complete until it is shared with those in the valley. Selfishness cost us the garden, but selflessness gains countless others a seat in the kingdom.

We must never forget how to transmit, how to talk, how to communicate, and how to care. These are our passports into the tough territory of tired and troubled souls, but they are sufficient to gain us entrance and a hearing. Inquiring minds want to know. They will meet us at every turn and juncture in the road. They want to know about this man named Jesus. It is our job to reveal him in such a way that their response becomes, "I want to give my life to Christ."

# 10

# AND THE GATES OF HELL SHALL NOT PREVAIL

And I say also unto thee, That thou are Peter, and upon this rock I
will build my church; and the gates of hell shall not prevail against it.

—*Matthew 16:18, KJV*

## PROMISE OF THE TWENTY-FIRST CENTURY

THROUGHOUT THE COURSE of history, defeat has on many
occasions looked inevitable. Moses was up against unbelievable
odds at the banks of the Red Sea, but God gave a blast of his nos-
trils, opened the waters, and the children of Israel walked on dry
land. Pharaoh's army was drowned. Elisha left Dothan and found
the city surrounded by an army. The lad with him feared for his
life, but Elisha prayed, "Lord, open his eyes,"and he saw the hors-
es and the chariots of fire. Daniel should have been eaten by lions.
The three Hebrew teens should have been burned to a crisp, but
when the smoke cleared and the dust settled they were alive and
their captors were dead. Biblical history may be too slanted for
some, but secular history tells the same story.

When the German armies bypassed the Maginot Line and invad-
ed France through the Netherlands and Belgium during World War
II, the British sent several divisions to northern France. After the
Germans trapped the British army and other Allied troops on the

beaches of Dunkirk, from out of nowhere the British naval fleet, joined by every vessel that could float, arrived, and over 300,000 British, French, and Belgian troops were evacuated to England.

In 1961, during our American civil rights movement and the summer of the Freedom Rides, an incident arose outside of the First Baptist Church in Montgomery, Alabama, where the Rev. Dr. Ralph David Abernathy was pastor and where Dr. Martin Luther King Jr. was scheduled to address a rally. The Freedom Riders were dedicated to the principles of change through nonviolent protest, yet they had been met with savage brutality throughout the South. Previous pleas to the federal government for protection had gone unheeded. An angry white mob had gathered at First Baptist Church and began throwing rocks through the church windows and attacking black citizens gathered outside the building. Just when it appeared that angry violence would once again be meted out against these protesters, federal marshals—who had been sent to an air force base close to Montgomery by the Attorney General—were sent to their rescue and the mob was dispersed.

Many attribute to luck, chance, coincidence, circumstances, or fatalistic orchestration the fact that when it looks as if we are down for the count and ready to throw in the towel, somehow victory breaks forth! What they do not seem to appreciate is that there is a God "who stands behind the shadows keeping watch above his own." God steps into the fray and makes his presence known. He does this because someone is out to get his people. Someone is out to destroy their destiny and halt their progress. Someone is out to get them to bow down at another altar and surrender to another flag. Someone is out to stop them in their tracks and to subvert the divine plan for their lives. The truth of the matter is that we are engaged in intense spiritual warfare.

Yet if the world sees and fears defeat, there must be one group that feels secure against all alarm, knowing that victory shall be theirs. This group is not a fraternal organization, civic club, or professional association. This assembly has a different compass and a different course. They believe beyond sight that God will not let them fall or fail, and that he will turn weeping into joy. That group is the church of the living Lord. This church is, in reality, people who know God for themselves. God takes care of his own, and he makes us this promise, "The gates of hell shall not prevail ... " *(Matthew 16:18, KJV).*

This promise was tucked away in a proclamation from the Master. It happened on the road outside Caesarea Philippi and is recorded in the Gospel of Matthew. Jesus had challenged his disciples with the question, "Who do people say the Son of Man is?" *(16:13, NIV).* Their response was that people were saying he was one of the prophets. He then pushed the question further by asking, "Who do you say I am?" *(16:15).* This question forced them to race through their memories and see if he matched any known entity. Was he a match for the prophets, or did he present something different? As they sought some way to express this new idea, Simon Peter rose with the declaration we know so well. "Simon Peter answered, 'You are the Christ, the Son of the living God'" *(16:16).*

Simon made his assessment and, even though it was radical, he voiced it and made it known. The Master then replied, "Blessed are you, Simon son of Jonah, for this was not revealed to you by man, but by my Father in heaven. And I tell you that you are Peter, and on this rock I will build my church, and the gates of Hades will not overcome it" *(Matthew 16:13–18, NIV).*

It is important to note the context of this question. For nearly three years Jesus had been in their midst. The truly unbelievable had happened. The once-in-a-lifetime moment had occurred. They had witnessed lepers healed, sight restored to the blind, broken hearts restored, and the dead brought back to life. Having seen such wonders, what conclusions had they reached? Simon Peter is the one to whom God gave the revelation. Jesus said to Peter, "Flesh and blood did not reveal this to you. I have been in your midst, and not everyone realized who I was, but my father revealed my true nature to you because you were open to believe it and to receive it" *(author's paraphrase).*

It is at this point that the Lord introduced a new concept: the church. Jesus said to Simon that he was, in this area, a rock. In this one area he had finally gotten it together. He reached a conclusion that the natural does not support. He blazed new territory. Jesus said to Simon, "In the area of believing that I am God, you cannot be moved, and upon that kind of bedrock I will build my church" *(author's paraphrase)*.

There is something very important to see here. We center on the revelation that Simon received, but what is equally important is the channel through which the revelation came. Simon Peter argued over who was the greatest, turned back people who wanted to see the Master, tried to stop Jesus from fulfilling his mission, and would deny the Master three times. Peter was flawed, but God gave him the ability to see what others could not see, in spite of every flaw. God gives revelation to flawed folks.

Imperfections do not stop us from fulfilling our work. Being less than perfect does not guarantee defeat. Shortcomings are facts of life, but the revelation that Jesus is ours is sufficient to help us overcome any imperfection and outlast any storm. This is the revelation that tilts the scales toward victory on our side. It is this wondrous truth that frees us from every yoke of bondage and defeats every maniacal scheme of the Adversary. When we embrace this truth, as blemished as we are, the power and the purposes of God come together in our lives in a new and mighty way. They serve to overpower our inner feelings of defeat as they revive us with the knowledge of what it means to belong to the Lord. Jesus tells a flawed man who is receiving revelation and favor in the midst of his faults this promise: The gates of hell shall not prevail.

## PITFALLS OF THE TWENTY-FIRST CENTURY

One of the problems we face in this new era is one we carry over from past ages: We have been coerced by the Prince of Darkness into believing that flaws make us unacceptable to God. The Bible is a book of people with imperfections who receive revelation and insight from God: David was flawed, but God gave him the hymns of the Old Testament; Paul was flawed, but God gave him the record for church growth. The truth of the matter is that we are all plagued by shortcomings of some sort, but somehow God looks beyond our faults and speaks to us in a way that gives us hope and destiny. God understands that if we can acknowledge our weaknesses, we can also acknowledge his strength. Those who cannot look at their own weaknesses will never be able to credit God with the wonders in their own lives. Sometimes we see the truly remarkable and still refuse to acknowledge it. We see progress but refuse to credit it to its source. We see growth but will not accept it. We misinterpret our enemy; we have looked at it only on a personal, one-on-one level. Our enemy is not flesh and blood. Our enemy is not in our imperfections, and it is not a name we speak or a face we see. We delude ourselves into thinking that we are engaged in an effort against people when the truth of the matter is that this is not about human beings. The strength of the struggles we often contend with should make us aware that its source is other than this world. We understand complex computer languages such as COBOL and comprehend intricate economic alliances such as cartels, but in the realm of spiritual evil our thinking is limited to terms such as *poltergeist* and *exorcist*. This war is a spiritual battle where the stakes are high and the weaponry far advanced. Forces are arrayed to stop our progress, turn back the hands of time, and take from us everything that God has given to us. Our enemy is none other than the archetype of evil, the prince of the air, the Adversary—the devil.

Unfortunately, we have seen evil as some kind of chaotic effort forced on individuals. Wickedness has such a field day with us because we have deluded ourselves into thinking that it is wild, unrelated, and unorganized. Evil has a plan; it proceeds along the continuum of its plan until its mission is accomplished. We are up against the calculated counsel of depravity that is entrenched in the very fabric of our lives. We are dealing with organized ideas and patterns of deception that have taken hold of and dominate our thinking. There is a connection between poor education, crime, drugs, and family decline. There is a correlation between cutting welfare and refusing to raise the minimum wage. There is a relationship between the dismantling of affirmative action and lowering the standard of living for a segment of disenfranchised Americans. The devil wants tension, resentment, and division, and he will use anything and anybody to accomplish it. He wants to divert our attention from the real issues of life and cause us to make war against one another.

## ADVENT OF THE TWENTY-FIRST CENTURY

We need to understand the image of Sheol that existed during the time of Jesus. Sheol was the shadowy place of the departed. The gates of Sheol opened only inwardly, which meant that those inside were not able to depart. It allowed only entrance, never exit. This was the imagery with which people lived. They were locked into the Sheols of life, and there was no way out. They had literally been captured and enslaved. They were behind bars. The walls that held them had gates that would never open.

The word *gate* was very important in Jesus' day. The elders actually sat at the gate and passed judgment on the affairs of the people. It was at the gate that judgment was rendered and counsel discerned. The city gate was where the ruling elders gathered to discuss the affairs of the town. Jesus is presenting the notion that the gates of hell, where evil counsel is devised, symbolize the collective counsel of evil. This is the organized center of the effort to defeat us. It represents an orchestrated attempt by the counsel of the wicked and the ungodly to destroy what God has destined.

Whether two thousand years ago or today, when we attack evil, we must attack its organized center. We must go after the counsel, the ideas that undergird the attack. The battle is in the minds of people; the "god of this age has blinded the minds of unbelievers,

so that they cannot see the light of the gospel of the glory of Christ …"
*(2 Corinthians 4:4, NIV)*. We are not going to make this world what
God wants it to be by coming over a wall or by knocking down a
tower. We must attack the gates of the seat of power, the center of
its authority. We must attack its core. We must attack with a new
idea. That is what freed the children of Israel from Egypt—a new
idea. The church was birthed from Jerusalem to Rome because of
a new idea. Jesus is that new idea. He has come to fellowship with
the lowest and the least and offers the highest and the best. He
offers a life in spite of mistakes and errors. He offers fellowship in
spite of foolishness. The world is crying for a new idea. The Lord
has given it to us, and we can trample those that sit at the gate with
the honesty of the Lord's grace and love. Those who sit at the gate
to maintain our captivity will watch from the ground our tri-
umphant ascent into the glorious destiny God has prepared for us.

Jesus says to his flawed fighters that the gates of hell shall not
prevail. They will be defeated. They will be dismantled. They will
be destroyed. They will be a reminder to all that the power of God
and his purpose for life shall forever stand in every millennium. The
gates may look imposing, but we are on the attack. One of the
greatest scenes in the New Testament is in Luke 4:14–30. Jesus
delivers his famous synagogue sermon, "The Spirit of the Lord is
upon me …" and the crowd reacts angrily. They lead him out of the
city to cast him down off the mountain. But on signal from his
Spirit, he stops in his tracts, turns around, and marches right back
through them. They divide, and he goes on his way.

The Master says to all warriors, "This is not a defensive fight;
rather, we are to be on the offense. Turn and look the enemy in the
eye and take back what he has stolen from you." Imperfect folks
who have made mistakes and continue to make mistakes must take
the battle to the enemy. "The gates of hell shall not prevail" is an
empowering statement! The enemy's gates will not hold out against
us; they will come down. The message of the Master is that these
gates, no matter how strong, cannot contain us. In fact, these are
the very gates he came to destroy. He will destroy them because we

will stand up, storm the gates, and break them open. This is the action that brings victory where defeat had planned a celebration. The power of the Holy Spirit who is aware of our every move is greater than any force that can be against us.

In this twenty-first century, it is time to take our fight to the world. It is the fifth round, and it is time to take the fight to our opponent. We wonder where the devil will strike next, but the reality is that he needs to worry about where we are going to strike next! Our faith has awakened, and the Adversary is aware that the power of God at work within us can bring down the gates. God has some choice places he wants us to stand. He has some major opportunities he wants to create for us, and the text says that we are going to break down that which has been trying to stop us. We are going to defeat the forces that fracture our communities and destroy lives. We are going to attack the Enemy on his own ground with the power of God.

The forces of this world fear spiritual conversation and spiritual vocabulary. We are going to fight with his name and his Word. John the Revelator understood this truth and wrote it in his record: "They overcame him by the blood of the Lamb and by the word of their testimony; they did not love their lives so much as to shrink from death" *(Revelation 12:11, NIV)*. No matter what others may say, at the name of Jesus, every knee shall bow. Faith teaches this, faith believes this, and faith sees it happen. There comes a moment when we have to stop trying to please everyone, because in doing so we dilute our strength. We have to declare that which is immutable in us; others will have to accept it or depart. The time for being disguised and cryptic is gone. "Stand fast therefore in the liberty wherewith Christ hath made us free, and be not entangled again with the yoke of bondage" *(Galatians 5:1, KJV)*.

We must stand up and boldly declare that we trust God. Stand and boldly speak about our convictions. Stand and cry aloud that we are flawed but his grace is amazing. Use his name, talk about his kingdom, lift up his standard, and watch the gates come down! Take the word of God as a sword, quote it, and rely upon it, for it is still sharper than any two-edged sword. The day of the battle has come. There is a rallying cry from the forces of Jehovah to turn back the hand of the enemy. He has been strong, but "… if God is for us, who can be against us?" *(Romans 8:31, NIV)*.

Our numbers may be small and our communities clustered. Our ideas may no longer be held in high regard. Our viewpoints may be relegated to a past era. Our beliefs may be challenged by a society that condemns but does not repent. Yet we rise to face the fight and to take the fight to the Adversary. We have been dormant long enough. The day of Jubilee has come; God has declared that his will shall be done. It is in him that we overcome all that would stop God's will in our lives. He is the one we must know and acknowledge and, in doing so, even the powers of darkness will crumble.

# 11

# CUT TO THE CHASE

When a Samaritan woman came to draw water, Jesus said to her, "Will you give me a drink?" (His disciples had gone into the town to buy food.)

The Samaritan woman said to him, "You are a Jew and I am a Samaritan woman. How can you ask me for a drink?" (For Jews do not associate with Samaritans.)

Jesus answered her, "If you knew the gift of God and who it is that asks you for a drink, you would have asked him and he would have given you living water."

"Sir," the woman said, "You have nothing to draw with and the well is deep. Where can you get this living water? Are you greater than our father Jacob, who gave us the well and drank from it himself, as did also his sons and his flocks and herds?"

Jesus answered, "Everyone who drinks this water will be thirsty again, but whoever drinks the water I give him will never thirst. Indeed, the water I give him will become in him a spring of water welling up to eternal life."

The woman said to him, "Sir, give me this water so that I won't get thirsty and have to keep coming here to draw water."

He told her, "Go, call your husband and come back."

"I have no husband," she replied.

Jesus said to her, "You are right when you say you have no husband. The fact is, you have had five husbands, and the man you now have is not your husband. What you have just said is quite true."

"Sir," the woman said, "I can see that you are a prophet."

—*John 4:7-19*, NIV

# PROMISE OF THE TWENTY-FIRST CENTURY

THE REALITY OF PREACHING in the twenty-first century is that what was traditionally called "classical preaching" no longer stands paramount within the range of sermon styles. There seems to be emerging an equally powerful approach to preaching, one normally seen in what are commonly defined as "charismatic" churches. The classical preaching style spends a great deal of time on the exegesis (analysis) and the exposition (explanation) of the sermon text. Its focus is understanding the truths that God's Word presents. The text leads to inferences and conclusions. It allows certain deductions to be made from the evidence presented in the Scriptures. It takes what God said and makes certain assertions.

The other preaching school does not focus on conclusions drawn from what God has said. Rather, it *declares* what God is saying to us in this day and age. It exegetes the text but then declares, "This is what the Lord says, now!"

It is becoming more and more clear that what we need in this era is a prophetic declaration that causes men and women to realize that God knows all about them and is ready and waiting to save and deliver them. We must step forward, declaring, "The Lord says...."

This truth becomes more and more clear when we consider the narrative of Jesus and the woman at the well. The Master was on his way to Galilee, and the Bible says that he had to go through Samaria. This was a region that Jews sought to avoid. Samaritans had been rejected by Ezra and separated from the Jews of pure lineage. They were outcast because their bloodline was not pure, and their rejection was a sore spot in the relationship between the two regions. In fact, the word spoken was that "the Jews and the Samaritans have no dealings." Yet the Master pursued that course and went through a region where opposition would present opportunity. Gifts shine brightest in the deepest darkness. This way would present its own challenges, but Jesus was prepared to go in that direction.

The Scriptures declare that Jesus arrived at the well of Jacob in the city of Sychar and sat down while his disciples went to town to purchase food. There, an interesting interchange took place that teaches all of us who are looking for a way to accomplish the Great Commission. This is a marvelous sight to envision. Jesus was seated at the well when a woman came to draw water. It was noon, and all the other women were back in their homes. She came when they left, because she was not welcomed in their company. Her lifestyle did not afford her a place in their midst.

The Master began the conversation with a request for water, and a coy, almost coquettish, interchange began. It appears that she was flirting with Jesus and had no idea with whom she was speaking. The serious and the beneficial were lost on her as she contemplated playing games with Jesus. This is so indicative of our age and the experiences that we have. We can be in such darkness that we do not identify our deliverance even when it is standing right in our face. We talk to people and seek to play games with them, laugh at them, or just turn them off. "Here comes the church boy ...There is the preacher man ... Here comes Miss Holy." The response and the comments are familiar to those who stop by the well and seek to become involved in another's life.

Jesus pushed the situation to a profound level when he said to her, "If you knew the gift of God and who it is that asks you for a drink, you would have asked him and he would have given you living water" *(John 4:10, NIV)*. The Master wanted to break through that tough veneer. He wanted to deal with her on a level that would lead to her deliverance and her victory. She was a haunted woman, but she had no sense that her deliverance had arrived.

This was a critical moment, because it lays out for us a blueprint for reaching the unreachable. Jesus moved from petty conversation and the request for a glass of water to something that made the woman stop in her tracks. He started talking about the woman's life. He said to her, "Go call your husband and come back" *(v. 16)*, to which she answered, "I have no husband" *(v. 17)*. Jesus then lowered the boom when he replied, "You are right when you say you have no husband. The fact is, you have had five husbands, and the one you now have is not your husband. What you have just said is quite true" *(vv. 17, 18)*.

It was at this point that the tone of the conversation changed. We go from flirtation to faith building. With the woman at the well, Jesus "cut to the chase." She declared, "Sir, I can see that you are a prophet" *(v. 19)*. In other words, he "read her." Her life was an open book before him. He spoke into her life a word that she knew was true and that he could have learned only from a higher power. She was talking smack, but when he spoke in the Spirit, she changed her attitude. When the moment concluded, she went running to town, telling everyone, "Come, see a man ..." *(v. 29)*.

What was it that changed defeat into victory? What was it that took a conversation going nowhere and set it on the road to glory? What was it that broke down the barrier between two races of people? It was the exercise of the gift of the Spirit. Talking in the Spirit and declaring what the Lord has said turned the moment around!

Thanks be to God, his word gives hope. There is an interesting word in the letter to the Ephesians. Paul writes, "... he gave some to be apostles, some to be prophets, some to be evangelists, and some to be pastors and teachers, to prepare God's people for works of service, so that the body of Christ may be built up ..." *(Ephesians 4:11, NIV)*.

Christ has, through his Spirit, given every era the tools and weapons to fight the darkness that seems to be enveloping the age. We are not to use our intellect, nor are we to rely on our reasoning power. The key to saving this age and bringing the world to Christ is to use our spiritual gifts. His promise to us is that he will give us gifts that will enable us to accomplish our task. Our gifts make the presence of God real and unavoidable. Do not be deceived! What will cause people to take notice of our witness—just as we see happening with the woman at the well—is our ability to declare what the Lord says and make God a *present* reality in their lives. The Lord has promised us the gifts that give us the power to declare the words of God that cut to the chase and open the world's eyes to the presence of the Kingdom. Such a prophetic declaration causes men and women to realize that God knows all about them and is ready—and waiting—to save and deliver them.

## PITFALLS OF THE TWENTY-FIRST CENTURY

There is a great revelation that comes to us from the Garden of Eden. When Adam and Eve were driven out and forced to live outside the place called Paradise, they discovered what it means to be outside of love. Those that came after them wrestled and struggled with the issue of love. Thousands of years later, in this millennium, the issue that marks our age is that we have felt unloved by the only one who can free us. The fall from the garden has left a cancer that worsens with each generation.

Though we have greater technology and have made strides in nearly every aspect of our lives, our existence is more chaotic and the confusion and divisions that exist are, without a doubt, widening. The news media remind us daily that this world is no friend to grace. The work environment continues to serve as a black cauldron whipping up a witch's terrorizing brew, and home for many is no longer the place where the heart is. The times have become hectic, and life has become frenzied.

Little children are growing up without sound teaching, the sons and daughters of parents who are but children themselves. There are gangs and gang bangers popping up in the most unheard-of places. The night culture is about to replace the day culture as the rules of civilization are twisted and bent. Ethics are situational, morality is debatable, and responsibility and accountability are transferable.

There are those who have never heard of the church, others who have never entered the church, and many that hold the church in contempt. Some walk past and believe it outdated. Others think that it is irrelevant and has no message for the trouble that we face. Some have reiterated Karl Marx's supposition that the church is the "opiate of the people," believing that we are just superstitious individuals who prefer to hide behind faith than to take responsibility for our lives. There are many who have no church rootage and who do not have any understanding of what the church is all about or who Jesus is.

To add insult to injury, at the other end of the spectrum there are those who are looking for a church but who are not looking for a savior. There are people who shop for churches as they do for groceries, looking to see where they can get the most for their money. They want a church that has a full map of programs, ministers to children, and has multiple services that are based on convenience. They have brought consumerism into the church and have, in the process, ignored the purpose of the church. Our consumption-generated society has people looking for what they can get, even at the expense of what they need. Too often churches fall into the trap of trying to be all things to all people but, in the process, win none.

We know we are called to witness to our family members and our friends who do not know Christ. We know that we must speak a word of truth and salvation to brothers and sisters who have become participants in a culture of death and violence so that they will forsake that lifestyle and follow Christ. God wants everyone saved, and we must step up to the plate and accomplish the task we are called to do. We know that we must not only speak the language of the era but we must also be able and willing to *declare* God's Word to the people. Yet the times are so foreboding and the world so suspecting, skeptical, and cynical that the possibility of succeeding seems to grow dimmer and more unattainable each day.

## ADVENT OF THE TWENTY-FIRST CENTURY

When the woman at the well heard the Savior tell her what she thought no strangers knew, she realized that he was, indeed, a prophet. It was what he spoke that made her listen. It was what he said that caused her to pay attention. It was what he presented that caused her to move in a different direction. Our problem in this age has been that we have tried to do everything and use everything except the one thing that will work. We have not used our anointing, our spiritual gifts, our power of declaration to bring people into the saving knowledge of our Lord. Indeed, the Lord does have a word to be spoken. This is important because the declaration of God speaks to our deepest issues.

He speaks to the deep and secret things in our heart and, by the very nature of speech, exposes them for what they really are. When the Master confronted the woman at the well with the word of knowledge, she had no defense against it, because it reached down into an area of pain that she kept hidden from view. She had made a mess of her life. She had had five husbands, each marriage had failed, and now she was living with a man. This was unheard of in her day. Her reputation was in the gutter, and her sense of worth had fallen off the chart. This was a sore spot in her life, and here was a man who did not know her, but who *did* know her. He had never met her, but he *had* met her. He had never been in her company, yet he knew her life story. And he was brave enough, daring enough, and Spirit filled enough to declare it to her! He did not talk behind her back; he came out in the open with a word she knew— one that she knew had to come from above.

When we are trying to win the world for Christ, we must let him use us to accomplish the task. Let him speak and we will watch others be saved. What draws them is his Word that is spoken to their pain and their deep, hidden areas. Many people have abandoned hope in God because they think he cannot handle their pain. However, when we speak to that pain with a word from the Lord, they realize that their hope comes from the Lord. The twenty-first century will be converted only when we speak the present word of the Lord and are willing to touch people at a deep and abiding level.

This kind of power does not operate like magic, nor is it employed on an emergency 911 basis. We have to cultivate listening to God's voice so that we can speak his Word. The Bible is right: "Faith comes from hearing the message, and the message is heard through the word of Christ" *(Romans 10:17, NIV)*. We have to speak the word of God into the situations that are binding people. Their freedom is contingent upon our ability to speak the word of the Lord that will liberate and set the captives free.

When we use this as the key, many of the miracles of the Master make even more sense. He spoke to the deepest hurt in their hearts. When the man was brought to Jesus on a stretcher, Jesus spoke to the man's real problem—sin. Everyone thought the brother was just bedridden from some illness, yet the truth was that sin had eaten him up and robbed him of even his hope. He expected Jesus to do a medical diagnosis and ask questions about his family history and his childhood illnesses. Instead, the Master goes to the one thing the brother feels is behind it all. He has not spoken it to another, but the Master says it to him. He says, "… your sins are forgiven…. Get up, take your mat, and go home" *(Matthew 9:2,6, NIV)*. The man did as he was told and walked away shouting. We must use our gifts, speak to the heart of the pain, and set the captives free!

The woman at the well was not expecting those prophetic words to fall from the lips of Christ. She flirted with him until he spoke, and then she listened with attention. Once the Master brought in the power of the Spirit, her defenses went down and her life began to change. We have to understand that when Jesus spoke, he spoke with authority, but he also spoke the truth in love. It was the twin force of authority and love that broke the chains that bound her. The Old Testament is about speaking the word with authority, but the New Testament witness of Jesus is that our declaration must be with love. We must speak the truth but do so with love. That is the mandate of the Master, because he knows it is our need for love that will enable us to embrace the Lord of love. We learn how to represent and manifest love by watching him. There is no better teacher on how to operate in both love and authority than Jesus. Even when he was stern, he was loving.

This is so important because we often divorce the two and associate with just one. There are those who speak with harsh authority and whose voices seem to command even the elements. Yet they are not capable of accomplishing what the Master did because authority by itself is not enough. Power and position are not enough to free the captives from the clutches of the Adversary. Conversely, we have encountered those whose words melt like butter but who do not seem to have the spine necessary to tackle hard issues and resistant forces. Life for them boils down to sentimentality and emotionalism. They do not understand that they must take back what the Enemy has stolen from them. We will not win this world for Christ with just harsh words and stern behavior. We will not break the devil's grip with a feeble faith that has no teeth. We must wed the two.

The church today needs to recapture this Jesus kind of love. We need authority to speak and love that undergirds what we say. The Master was not angry because the woman had horrible morals; he wanted to help liberate her from the inner pain that caused her to live her life in that manner. His aim was her deliverance and liberation. We must not lose track of that. The Adversary causes us to focus on the dark sides of people's lives, but the Master is out to lead them to the light.

There is an interesting story in the eighth chapter of the Gospel of John. A woman caught in the act of adultery was brought to Jesus to be judged. The leaders wanted her to be stoned and wanted the Master to validate their verdict. She had broken the law, and the Law of Moses called for her to be stoned. The Master, however, used his authority in a different way. With the woman standing before him, he said, "He that is without sin among you, let him first cast a stone at her" *(John 8:7, KJV)*. One by one they all slipped away. He looked at the woman who felt that her life was over and that she would have no tomorrows and said, "Where are those thine accusers? ... Go, and sin no more" *(vv. 10-11)*. He used authority and love; she received a new lease on life.

The need of the day is to stop trying to hide our pain and mask our problems with defensive tactics. We need to abandon the practice of holding onto the lies that have been crippling us. It is time to let the Word penetrate our hearts and restore the wholeness we have lost. The text describing the woman at the well says that the Word had so much power that the woman left her pots and *ran* to town to share her good news. Jesus cut to the chase and stopped her in her tracks with a powerfully prophetic Word. His Word spoke to her pain, and she made a conscious decision not to run away from the truth. The Master spoke the God Word into her life, and she chose to face what he said and be blessed by what he could do. She did not go berserk; she did not become infuriated. She did not protest the claim; she did not do verbal battle with Jesus. She opened herself to his words, embraced the truth, and let him minister to her.

The Word lets us take the masks off and see ourselves for who we really are. The call of the prophet Isaiah stresses this. He was in the temple when he saw a vision of the Lord, high and lifted up. It was out of that experience that he really began to see himself. He said, "Woe is me ... because I am a man of unclean lips" *(Isaiah 6:5, KJV)*. He stopped wearing the mask. Understand that the soul wants deliverance. It is just waiting on the right word to start the process. When we hear that Word, the soul rises and the spirit takes control.

Calvary is Jesus' greatest statement. On Calvary he spoke the loudest and the clearest. He made a statement that speaks to all of us. At Calvary, we take off our false faces and hang up our masks. At the cross, the player becomes the penitent, the liar becomes the truth seeker, the criminal becomes the converted, the sinner becomes the saint, the whoremonger becomes the worshiper, the scoundrel becomes the singer, the fearful become the faithful, and the rebel becomes the reverent. It is at the cross that we are made whole and alive as his Word breaks down every barrier in our lives.

We no longer have to cover up our lives, because his prophetic Word assures us that he already knows all about us! We can open up because he has made the first step. He understands, and he has come to set our souls free. He speaks the Word we need to hear.

# 12

# A VISION OF THINGS TO COME

Then I saw a new heaven and a new earth, for the first heaven and
the first earth had passed away, and there was no longer any sea.
I saw the Holy City, the new Jerusalem, coming down out of heaven
from God, prepared as a bride beautifully dressed for her husband.

*—Revelation 21:1-2, NIV*

## PROMISE OF THE TWENTY-FIRST CENTURY

THE SCIENCE OF OPHTHALMOLOGY offers members of
the faith community an interesting way of understanding the state
of "vision" in the church. There are two basic eyesight conditions
that most of us know well: farsightedness and nearsightedness.
Farsightedness is the condition where, to be as simplistic as possible, people can see far away but have difficulty with things that
are close by. They wear glasses to read and to clearly see things
that are within a few feet of their eyes. Nearsightedness is the
reverse. Nearsighted people can see things that are right in front
of them clearly, but they have tremendous difficulty focusing on
things at a distance. They see well what is close at hand, but they
cannot see, with the same clarity, things that are far off.

Transferring this terminology to the realm of religion, the church
can be said to be suffering from a form of *spiritual* nearsightedness.
We can see things up close and dissect them to minutia, but we have
a problem looking to the horizon and seeing what God is calling for
in the days that are to come. We are good at the now, but we have

not mastered the "not yet." We cannot see that far, cannot focus on that distant picture. We cannot conceive where we ought to be going.

This is true not just of the church; it is also true of church people. We can see clearly where we are. We understand our present position, but we have a hard time looking into the future and seeing what will unfold for us. Even if we see it, we seldom embrace it. We have a hard time believing that it will happen for us. Yet the future is not only waiting for us, it is calling to us. It is summoning us to step up and start to make it happen. We need "vision correction." We require spiritual laser surgery in order to see properly. God has so much in store for us as we live our lives and plot our courses in the twenty-first century. He has great things planned and prepared for us. It is, however, essential that we believe in and head in that direction. The church and Christians must believe that we have entered a season of unparalleled challenge. We must trust God that the future does, indeed, belong to us.

God wants us to look to the future and believe what is awaiting us. He wants us to see the challenges he is laying out for us and the blessings that are in their wake. There is service in the future, but there is also a shout. There is work, but there is also witness. There is much to be accomplished, but there is great rejoicing. What God wants us to do is to move beyond our encumbrances and have a vision of things to come!

A definitive text regarding the nature of "vision" is found in the Book of Revelation. If anyone thinks that the Revelation of John the Divine was written from the comfort of a couch while enjoying the magic moments of life, that person is greatly mistaken. This is not the fruit of meditation or an intentional manuscript written on a ministerial retreat. It is the work of a man who thought that his future was bleak and that the future was without hope. John was exiled to the lonely, craggy island of Patmos, a place reserved for those whose days were numbered. John is away from the fire of the faith; his preaching tours have ended. His leading of the worship services is over. His fellowship with the saints has been terminated. This is his lot. This is his plight. This is his life.

What is so interesting is the fact that it is from Patmos that John receives this revelation, this apocalyptic message of the future of humanity and God's role in that future. It is from Patmos, where the future is bleak, that we receive the revelation of a future that is glorious, enchanting, and inspiring. We need not count out our Patmos moments! They may be the very events that give us the revelation we need. That's the way God works, using the least likely places and the least likely people to put us in line for what he has for us.

For examples from Scripture, we need look no further than Ezekiel, who was sitting with the other exiles by the river Chebar when God gave him a vision and called him into greater service. Elijah, the prophet of God, was in a cave in Mount Horeb, bemoaning his plight and feeling sorry for himself. A glorious moment of victory had turned into a time of great despair. His heart was broken and his spirit was heavy. He was ready to give up, and he had left Samaria. He traveled far to reach Horeb, and when he was in a state of deep depression, God spoke to him. He did not speak in a loud voice but in a still, small voice. When Elijah left Horeb, he left on fire, and the fire never again failed.

It is the lonely places that give birth to the great visions. It is in the place of abandonment that we find the vision of fellowship. When we are at our lowest, God takes us to his highest.

John is on the island for his defense of the faith, and now God opens the curtains of heaven's theater and allows John to see how it shall all end. He sees a new heaven and a new earth. He sees the redemption of all that has been corrupted. He sees a glorious new world for those who love the Lord. He sees his labor's reward. He sees the fruit of his efforts. He realizes that there is no need to be "… weary in well doing: for in due season we shall reap, if we faint not" (*Galatians 6:9, KJV*). He sees the old order pass away and a new order emerge. It will come because people like him fight to make it happen and do not surrender in spite of all the obstacles in their way. God lets John see what will come to pass and how his suffering shall be vindicated. In theology, we call this apocalyptic; John just called it a vision. He saw something that made his spirit

**101**

come alive, that resuscitated his failing and faltering hope and caused him, once again, to be encouraged.

It is vision that keeps us going. The Bible says it best in Proverbs 29:18 *(KJV)*: "Where there is no vision, the people perish...." It is vision that makes us take up new challenges and struggle against oppressive forces. The vision of a society not marked by the differences of race and gender has been the driving force behind the civil rights movements that have brought us breakthroughs such as equal housing and the voting rights bill. The vision of the home, the children in college, the mission assignment, the new church, the choir concert, the baby's birth, the day of graduation—these are all part of God's great drama of redemption. We must see beyond the horizon; the day-to-day struggles and situations must yield to a higher vision of the future where there is victory and success. Vision is not taught in schools. It is not a class in the university. Yet it is the underlying and undergirding force that moves history.

We are on our way somewhere, and we—the people of faith—know that "somewhere" to be the dwelling place of God. We are on our way to the end of history and the fulfillment of eternity. We are on our way back to Eden. Paradise lost will be paradise regained. This is the Christian hope and calling. This is the vision that propels the saints of God. Vision is for the mother who is beset by the circumstances of life. Vision is for the father who feels as if life only makes demands and offers so little in return. Vision is for the youngster who is struggling to maintain a sense of sanity while living in a situation marked by chaos and confusion. Vision opens locked doors and revives the creative spirit. It makes us feel as if we can take on life and, this time, come out victorious.

God's steadfast promise to us is that he will provide a vision for the future! He does not just dry our eyes and calm our fears. He does not just provide food and shelter. He does not just raise up friends and comrades. He also provides vision. He shows us what we need to see. He gives us a glimpse of things to come. He gives us a view of a better day, a brighter horizon, and our blessed fulfillment. God gives to each of us a piece of his cosmic picture. He gives us a slice of the grand plan and says, "Go for it!"

What we see as vision is, in God's eternity, already a reality. He has not only designed the plan; in his eternity, he has executed it. He shows us what is to come for us, but it has already happened for him. We wonder "if," and God knows "it shall." God gives us vision to motivate us toward the desired end. He lets us peek at the end of the chapter, at the last page, and then rise up to make it happen. God is offering a future, and it has his blessing on it.

## PITFALLS OF THE TWENTY-FIRST CENTURY

The person who expects a straight line from vision to victory is woefully mistaken. The Adversary, the Prince of Darkness, the Deceiver of the Brethren, waits at every turn to thwart the plan of God for our lives. He attempts to discourage us by putting obstacles in our path. He attempts to frighten us by presenting strong opposition. He is out to test and prove our mettle and to see us do as Adam and Eve did: fall away from our destiny. The Adversary takes his time to make us feel as if the vision will not come to pass.

But what we receive as vision has already been completed in God's reality. God gives us the vision surrounded by his promise and protection, but as that vision enters the realm of our reality, it is attacked by the realities of this world. The Adversary adds the burden to the blessing. Many of us have had this happen to us. We knew what God had planned for us. We knew the outcome, but something came along to put us in a tailspin. That something is the work of the Adversary, and his aim is to throw us off course.

We have become bound by our history, afraid of our past, and well aware of our previous mistakes, but God has considered all of that and has still prepared a great blessing for our future. Many of the Lord's people are just going through the motions of living. They want better and wish for better, but they are afraid to "envision" better. They keep their dreams like novels that are good to read but have no basis in reality. They know the Scripture declares in Mark 9:23 *(NIV)* that "everything is possible for him who believes," but actually believing it is another matter.

For so many, life has depleted our energy to such an extent that we often fear we will not hold up under the strain. We have been so battered by the pressures of life that we abandon the hope and the vision simply because it feels safer. We feel as if we, too, are on the island of Patmos. We feel as if our lives are empty and without purpose or plan. We feel as if we have been relegated to the loneliest areas of life and are being forced to endure it alone. We do not dream because we believe that dreams do not come true.

It is precisely in the direction of despair and hopelessness that our destiny and our future are found. It is precisely in the direction of blindness and pain that we break the chains and shackles that have held us captive for years. We can struggle to get an education, even if there are no scholarships. We can break out of the cycle of poverty, even if we work at minimum wage with no benefits. We can overcome generational curses, even if family members think we are crazy. God will empower us to go through whatever obstacles are placed in our paths and attain the vision he has given us. God strengthens us to endure and to hold out; no force is strong enough to break the grip he has on our lives.

## ADVENT OF THE TWENTY-FIRST CENTURY

Note carefully these words of John as he describes his revelation: "On the Lord's Day I was in the Spirit, and I heard behind me a loud voice like a trumpet, which said: 'Write on a scroll what you see and send it to the seven churches: to Ephesus, Smyrna, Pergamum, Thyatira, Sardis, Philadelphia and Laodicea'" *(Revelation 1:10-11, NIV)*. Note his words carefully. He is on Patmos, and the mood is anything but uplifting; but it is the Lord's Day. He does not let anything interfere with his date with God. It is the day of worship, the day of praise, the day of celebration. Christ Jesus has broken the bonds of death and risen to life. Christ Jesus is alive and lives forevermore. In spite of his plight, John is gripped by the victory of Jesus and worships on the Lord's Day. The knowledge of the resurrection gives him hope.

Even when we drop to the lowest level of despair, the celebration of the Lord's Day tells us Christ has defeated every foe. That is why we leave church feeling better and revived. We have been reminded that Jesus is alive and that his victory is extended to us. God honors those who come before him dragging their baggage behind them, however heavy it may be. He honors those who are daunted by the pressures at the workplace, the severe agony of illness, the lack of money, the absence of transportation, or the need of acceptable attire, and make a way to honor the Lord's Day. John knew that if he was to make it through his Patmos, he needed the constant reminder of the work of the living God that worship offers us.

The text is very definite as it relates to John's posture on Patmos on the Lord's Day. We was *in the Spirit*. This is no minor inclusion; in fact, the weight of the revelation rests on this assertion. It was Sunday, the Lord's Day, and John was in the Spirit. This is a phrase that many are fearful to use or embrace, yet here is one of the Lord's followers boldly declaring that he was in the Spirit. It was Sunday; he was in worship. What other posture was he to have? The only way to worship is in the Spirit. John understood this fundamental truth: It is the *Comforter* who ushers us into the presence of God. Those people who claim to worship apart from the Spirit are only "attending" worship. This is not about body actions and particular movements, either. This is about a state of being and consciousness.

When we enter into worship—whether it is in a church or in our home, at a worship center or at the workplace, at the altar or in our automobile—we must first enter into that sacred and secret place in our hearts where his Spirit abides and reigns. This is where we are able to commune with him. John said he was in the Spirit, which means his consciousness, his thoughts, and his feelings were all influenced by the presence of the Spirit—the Paraclete. On that lonely island, John's feelings and emotions, his thoughts and perceptions, his understanding and reasoning were all under attack. But in the Spirit, all three were strengthened, quickened, and given power. The Holy Comforter does a transformation work on the areas of our lives where we need help. The Spirit does not just bring us into worship, it brings the results of worship into us. The psalmist lifts up one of those rewards: "In the presence of the Lord is fullness of joy, and at his right hand are blessings forevermore" *(Psalm 16:11, author's paraphrase)*.

It is time for those of us who are twice born to realize that we need to be in the Spirit. This is not denominational language; this is the word of God. The blessing of being in his presence and having the Comforter make intercession for us is absolutely incalculable. He is truly "able to do immeasurably more than all we ask or imagine, according to his power that is at work within us" *(Ephesians 3:20, NIV)*. Being in the Spirit opens the door for this blessing. It was out of this that John received the revelation. While he was in the Spirit, he was open to what God wanted him to hear and see. Others have given similar testimonies: Paul said he was caught up into the third heaven and saw things about which it is unlawful to speak; Isaiah said he was in the temple and saw the Lord himself, high and lifted up.

The Paraclete allows us to transcend the boundaries of our humanness, escape the confines of our narrow existence, and soar into the reality that is God in both time and eternity. John saw the coming of the end because he was in the Spirit. If we want to have a vision of things to come, then we need to allow God to show us what only spiritual eyes can see.

When John's spiritual eyes were opened, he saw "a new heaven and a new earth." He saw things change; he saw the world, as he knew it, pass away. John saw God's plan. John's vision had many parts, but it culminated in a new world. The revelation that John received was filled with wars and struggles, but it ends with a new heaven and a new earth. In order to get to the new heaven and the new earth, various tribulations must be endured. This is God's way of letting us know that every vision we are given comes with some conflict incorporated into it. Vision never comes without an accompanying burden that must be overcome. Yet the strength of the revelation is that God is the one who overcomes and gives the church strength to triumph. In other words, we have help. This is the power of the vision God gives to us. We have the strength and the authority of God behind us; we are not in this alone.

Finally, when John received a vision of things to come, the fulfillment of the revelation brought great rejoicing in heaven and on earth. Whenever we complete the work that God has given us and whenever we arrive at the place God wants us, we have helped to hasten his kingdom. Our steps and stops give him glory and help to advance his kingdom. In fact, John ends his record with one phrase: "Come, Lord Jesus" *(Revelation 22:21, NIV)*. The entire creation is awaiting his return. The world will be changed, life will be redefined, and the kingdom of God will reign forever. This was John's hope, but we have that hope, too.

We must be guided by that hope and realize that the world is made better by our efforts. Whenever that mother on welfare sees the vision of breaking out of the cycle and stands forth to accept the challenge, there is rejoicing. Whenever that young man decides that he can make it through college even if he has to work, there is rejoicing. Whenever that family believes that it can be reestablished and works to make it happen, there is rejoicing. God has a smile put on his face whenever his vision inspires us and encourages us to action. Vision will—

- turn families around;
- destroy the yoke of poverty;
- vanquish racism and sexism;
- clean up neighborhoods;
- restore the lives of children;
- lift a fallen person to new heights in Christ Jesus!

John saw the vision of a new heaven and earth; that same vision propels and motivates us. We know that one day this life will be over and we shall see God as he is. John's vision moves in the right direction. God is showing what he has for us. It is ours to accomplish.

# 13

# SO MUCH FOR SO LITTLE

The Lord will grant you abundant prosperity—in the fruit of your womb, the young of your livestock and the crops of your ground—in the land he swore to your forefathers to give you. The Lord will open the heavens, the storehouse of his bounty, to send rain on your land in season and to bless all the work of your hands. You will lend to many nations but will borrow from none. The Lord will make you the head, not the tail. If you pay attention to the commands of the Lord your God that I give you this day and carefully follow them, you will always be at the top, never at the bottom.

*—Deuteronomy 28:11–13, NIV*

## PROMISE OF THE TWENTY-FIRST CENTURY

THE HISTORY OF THE WORLD is marked by war. In the final one hundred years of the twentieth century, we witnessed Desert Storm, the invasions of Grenada and Panama, the Falkland Islands War, the Vietnam War, the Korean War, the Communist revolution, World War II, and World War I. These conflicts that have given markers to modern history have centered around territory, politics, trade, and *freedom*. From the earliest annals of time until present history, humanity has sought to realize its dreams of freedom. Freedom has been a cause worth fighting and dying for: the Bolsheviks wanted freedom from the Romanovs, the Czechoslovakian people wanted freedom from their communist oppressors, and the student protestors in Beijing's Tiananmen

Square wanted freedom from oppression and a liberalization of Chinese political policies. The South African people wanted liberation from the oppressive grip of apartheid. Even in America, the revolutionary war was fought for the freedom of the nation, the Civil War was fought to assure the freedom of all its citizens, and in the 1960s the streets ran red with blood as African Americans cried out for equal justice and the freedom to attain their fair share of the American dream.

Freedom is an awesome prize, but it is not obtained without great price. The blood of the martyrs cries out as a witness to the high cost of freedom. The words of Frederick Douglass ring out for our embrace, "Power concedes nothing except upon demand."[1] James Weldon Johnson wrote this thought into our anthem:

> We have come over a way that with tears has been watered.
> We have come, treading our path through the blood of the
> slaughtered. Out from the gloomy past, till now we stand at last
> Where the white gleam of our bright star is cast.[2]

Even at such a price, people want to be free. This does not mean freedom from responsibility; that is an irresponsible request. We want to be free to achieve what we know we are destined to accomplish. We want to spread our wings like the eagle and chance the currents of the wind. We want to go higher than we have ever journeyed and deeper than we have ever imagined. Most of us would have to admit that we would gladly shed some of our excess baggage and concerns for an opportunity to put our dreams into action. We know that, given the chance, we can become something greater than we are. Indeed, the saddest of people are those whose dreams have not just been deferred but defeated and destroyed.

Yet there is a word found in the Bible that demands our attention as we consider freedom and its costs. It is the reporting of Moses about the progress of the children of Israel. They were nearing the moment of their entrance into the Promised Land. The days of their wandering were nearing an end. The time of their travel was about to give way to the blessing of their arrival. They had reached the appointed place, and their new future was about to commence. What is important here are the facts that surround this passage.

First, Israel left Egypt because God set her free. She did not have to fight for her freedom. She did not have the compound burden of oppression and the struggle to be liberated. She only had to sit and watch while the God of her fathers did for her what others before and since have had to do for themselves. Second, her journey had been made bearable because God had guided her. His pillar and cloud had served her well and kept her from anything that could have destroyed her. Third, she was now ready to enter the land, and God gave her a promise and a guarantee. The people were promised—

■ abundant prosperity;
■ the heavens will be opened;
■ they will be lenders to the world;
■ they will have no need to borrow; and
■ they shall be the head and not the tail—leaders, not just followers.

To quote a familiar saying, "It doesn't get any better than that." God promised to be the greatest benediction they could imagine. They would not face one force that could rewrite the promise that God had made. The days of their oppression were over, and the days of their blessing were to begin. God was giving out goodies that make even the most disappointed and weary people rethink their position. This is so much! Moreover, the only thing that he required was that Israel obey his word and follow his commands. All he asked was that the people remain faithful to him. "If you pay attention to the commands of the Lord your God that I give you this day and carefully follow them, you will always be at the top, never at the bottom" *(Deuteronomy 28:13, NIV)*. He offered so much for so little!

This promise is not just for Israel but for every believer who takes God at his word and makes it applicable to every situation in life. This offer is for us in the twenty-first century. This promise is representative of the promises God made for all ages. There are over 8,000 of them in the Bible. They cover every subject imaginable.

They address our needs, our wants, our fears, our hopes, our frustrations, and our desires. These promises are not limited warranties. They do not stay in effect for the first thirty or ninety days of our salvation; they stand for the duration. They hold their verity until their need has been replaced by God's eternal presence. He makes unconditional, open-ended promises and says the only thing necessary to keep them in effect is obedience to his word and his will.

## PITFALLS OF THE TWENTY-FIRST CENTURY

Yet as we read the history of Israel, we see that she never fully realized this promise. One might wonder if God promised more than he could deliver or if an overexcited writer went further than God declared. Israel never experienced the fullness of this promise. This inability to gain so much for so little can cause us to rethink the promise, but then we realize that the problem is not the promise; the problem is in the people to whom it has been given. Shakespeare said, "The fault lay not in our stars but in ourselves." My mother said it this way, "There ain't no failure in God. He's the same yesterday, today, and forevermore." God defeated Pharaoh; God led them out to freedom; God guided them through the wilderness; God brought them to the land. If the failure is not in God, then why did they give up so much when it cost them so little?

This question is not just an Old Testament question. This is a question for every age, even this twenty-first century. Many of us today have missed the promise. We, too, have fallen short of the great invitation of God. We have been at the back of the train and the bus. We have been like street urchins scratching out a living. Too often we have been the ones on the team named "misery," just fighting to get into the playoffs. We live in an age when people will believe anything negative. The scandal media is able to maintain its existence because people have a love for anything negative. We despise hope and look for the next wind of adversity to blow.

We want to see the mistakes of the righteous; we want to see the faithful flawed. This kind of mentality makes us skeptical of anything and anyone who comes with a positive message and a word of hope. We are more prone to listen with cynicism and skepticism than we are to accept and believe.

The truth of the matter is that many of us have missed the promise. There are those of us who claim to believe but have never been able to launch out on faith. We hear about tithing, serving, risk taking, and life changes; we hear about coming out of bondage. We want to experience and take part in all these things, but we cannot bring ourselves to make the first step. Why are we good at hearing and poor at applying? We are all guilty. From the pulpit to the pew, we have all heard his word and followed our own desires. We have a problem yielding to another, even if the other is God. What happened? There must be a reason we have forfeited so much that costs and requires so little. The millionaire has come to our door, and we have found a reason not to answer.

The answer is found in the fact that, just like the children of Israel, we have never been willing to put God to the test. We do not believe that God will do what he said he would do. We do not believe he is powerful enough to correct our type of problem; we transfer our own fallibility to him. We have not been willing to launch out on faith and see if God would back up his Word. Churches are filled with people hearing the Word, but the admonition of James 1:22 *(KJV)* is that we become "… doers of the word, and not hearers only…." Hearing is a cognitive activity, but doing is a kinetic and manipulative activity. We learn about God not only through what we hear; our understanding of God is expanded by what we *do*. We are willing to hear and shout, but the acid test is not in the shout but in the living.

From little children to adults, we have this instinctive desire to rebel and fight against what is commanded. Children look for ways to skirt the commands and directives of their parents. Even as we reach maturity, we still rebel at the thought of being told what to do. This was Israel's real problem. They could not have their cake and eat it, too. God said the promises were theirs, but they must be obedient. In the process of their disobedience, they forfeited the blessings that were promised. The Bible can be read and interpreted using rebellion as a filter. From that which was before creation—Satan—to that which was the crown jewel of creation—humanity—rebellion has dogged the grace of God.

## ADVENT OF THE TWENTY-FIRST CENTURY

"If you fully obey the Lord your God and carefully follow all his commands I give you today, the Lord your God will set you high above all the nations on earth. All these blessings will come upon you and accompany you if you obey the Lord your God: You will be blessed in the city and blessed in the country" *(Deuteronomy 28:1–3, NIV)*.

God says that if we make the first step, he will make the second step. God says we are called to be at the head of the class, the top of the list, and the start of the show. We are his children and the sheep of his pasture. We are blessed in the cities and in the suburbs. We are blessed on the mountain and in the valley. We are blessed everywhere we turn. But we must obey God!

What does it mean to obey God?
- Love your brother and sister.
- Honor your body as the temple of God.
- Wives, submit to your husbands.
- Husbands, love your wives as Christ loved the church.
- Children, honor your parents.
- Do not lie.
- Do not covet that which belongs to another.
- Do not kill.
- Love the Lord with all your heart, mind, and soul.
- Honor the Sabbath and keep it holy.
- Help the weak.
- Defend the widows and orphans.

- Do good to them that hate you.
- Be merciful, a peacemaker, and a witness for the Lord.

These are but a few, but they call us to bend our will and allow his grace to change us into the likeness of Jesus Christ. Obedience is based in the fundamental question, "Do you really want to be like Christ?" Israel had a problem with obedience because it would not allow itself to be reshaped in the image God desired. Our rebellion costs us more than the promises and the treasures. It costs us the image of God in our lives. It costs us the change in personality that would bring us closer to God than we ever imagined possible.

God is offering us so much, and it costs us so little. There is more that God has to offer: the secret things still belong to God, and they will be revealed and seen for centuries to come. He has something better than anything that could be imagined. Humanity has done more than just refuse to take God at his word. Humanity has defied God and, through sin, ruptured its relationship with him. Our disobedience brought us the pain and suffering we endure in the world. Our sin set the world against itself and caused even creation to suffer. We could not fix what we damaged; we could not restore what we had broken.

Yet God was still willing to do so much for us. He sent his Son in the form of sinful flesh, and he suffered for us. He came to show us the way and took unto himself all the sins of the world. He endured the agony of the cross that we might be able to say, "Abba, Father!" Now, because of his death, we are heirs of the kingdom; we are reborn, repentant, restored, saved, sealed, sanctified, and justified. And one day we shall be glorified. In return, he asks only that we let our light shine so that others might see our good works and glorify our heavenly Father. He asks that we believe that he is the Savior of the world. He asks that we confess with our mouths and believe in our hearts that God has raised Jesus from the dead.

This word is true: He will honor those who honor him. When Eric Liddell of Scotland refused to run in the 100-yard dash in the Olympic Games of the 1920s because it was a Sunday, he shocked the entire world. The British thought his action unspeakable, but

God knew he was honoring the word to give God praise on the Lord's Day. The world watched Liddell obey God and then saw God bless him. He ran in the 400-yard race and ran like the wind. In the process, he captured the gold medal for the event. He honored God, and the Lord made him the top and not the bottom, the head and not the tail.

We are being challenged to believe and then to receive. We must take God at his word and believe him for what he has purposed, promised, and prepared for us. God will not fail. He will open the windows of heaven and pour out his blessings on our lives. This is the word and the will of God for his people. This is the promise for the faithful.

---

**Notes**

1. *Frederick Douglass. Life and Times of Frederick Douglass (1881).*
**2.** *"Lift Every Voice and Sing." Words by James Weldon Johnson. Reprinted in Songs of Zion (Nashville: Abingdon Press, 1981), 32.*

# 14

# FAITH AND THE FURNACE

King Nebuchadnezzar made an image of gold, ninety feet high and nine feet wide, and set it up on the plain of Dura in the province of Babylon. He then summoned satraps, prefects, governors, advisers, treasurers, judges, magistrates and all the other provincial officials to come to the dedication of the image he had set up. So the satraps, prefects, governors, advisers, treasurers, judges, magistrates and all the other provincial officials assembled for the dedication of the image that King Nebuchadnezzar had set up, and they stood before it. Then the herald loudly proclaimed, "This is what you are commanded to do, O peoples, nations and men of every language: As soon as you hear the sound of the horn, flute, zither, lyre, harp, pipes and all kinds of music, you must fall down and worship the image of gold that King Nebuchadnezzar has set up. Whoever does not fall down and worship will immediately be thrown into a blazing furnace."

*—Daniel 3:1-6, NIV*

## PROMISE OF THE TWENTY-FIRST CENTURY

KARL MARX, THE THINKER behind communism, described religion as the opiate of the people. In his mind, religion held people back and kept them from confronting the virulent forces of life. Governments have often feared religions and the impact they have on life. Orthodox Muslims threw out the Shah of Iran in the 1970s, and Hindus brought the British Empire to its knees in India in the 1940s.

Yet the truth of the matter is that it is not religion that produces these kinds of changes; it is religious people who live by the faith they profess. Religion in itself is never the source of the conflict, for religion is, at best, just a set of teachings and agreed-upon practices. The source of tension does not come from a building that carries the name of a church or a denomination. It comes when men and women begin to live what they believe and declare that they are on the Lord's side. At family reunions and company picnics, it is not religion that causes arguments. It is religious people who are determined to hold onto what they profess and confess.

People who take their faith seriously will always find that confrontation of one sort or another is awaiting them just around the corner. Faith can and does get us into trouble. The different drum that Thoreau mentioned is a constant source of difficulty for those who are earnest about what they believe. The news reported a sad but telling story that came out of the student massacre in Columbine, Colorado, just before the beginning of the twenty-first century. A young girl of seventeen was confronted by one the young terrorists and asked if she believed in God. In the murderers' eyes, the "correct" answer would have been no, but this young woman did not give that answer. With a gun pointed at her head and facing imminent death, she responded in the affirmative and the gunman shot her dead. Her death, tragic though it is, reinforced the fact that our faith—those gut-claimed beliefs that feed and nurture our lives—will cause us to make choices that come at high prices. She died, but the testimony of her conviction will live on. She could not renounce her faith and live a happy life, so she chose to hold onto her faith and claim an eternal reward.

Our faith teaches us in Mark 8:36 *(KJV)*, "For what shall it profit a man, if he shall gain the whole world, and lose his own soul?" The Scripture says it best: "That the trial of your faith, being much more precious than of gold that perisheth, though it be tried with fire, might be found unto praise and honour and glory at the appearing of Jesus Christ" *(1 Peter 1:7, KJV)*. The truth of the matter is that we who hold our faith dear are compelled to take a stand

**117**

and lift our voices. We try to be quiet and not rock the boat, but on more occasions than we care to discuss, we find ourselves rising up and taking a stance because there is a fire building inside of us. The prophet Jeremiah said it is like "… a burning fire shut up in my bones …" *(Jeremiah 20:9, KJV)*. We seem to develop a case of the "can't help its" and before we know it, we are speaking what we believe. Many of us can attest to the fact that such behavior has cost us friends, invitations, and even problems with our families and on our jobs. It is serious, and it can be very dangerous to proclaim the Lord and say, "for God I live and for God I die."

This is crucial and critical because, as we navigate our way through this twenty-first century, we have to be people who stand for something. This thought becomes even more gripping as we read the account of the Jewish exiles in Babylon, in particular the record of Hananiah, Mishael, and Azariah, whom we know as Shadrach, Meshach, and Abednego. The backdrop of this story is an exiled people trying to maintain faith in a distant land. They have been captured by a nation stronger than themselves and forced into captivity. In the midst of their struggle, they find the faith to fight against assimilation and ultimate destruction. God allows them to be purged in order to be developed. Their witness is refined like gold because their faith has been tested and found worthy.

Religious confrontation is normally over idolatry—putting something else in the place of God. This is the bedrock, the touchstone, the centerpiece of the problem. It does not matter where we are, whenever idolatry rises, conflict and confrontation are not far away. King Nebuchadnezzar built an idol, and the drama began. He ordered a festive and grandiose celebration, at which time all would bow down to the golden idol. He sought to make his understanding of his false god normative for everyone. He did this by declaring that everyone had to bow to his god; everyone had to worship his god. Regardless of an individual's faith, when the music sounded each person had to recognize the king's god as the true god. It was at this point that the three Hebrew teenagers ran into trouble. It was all right for the king to have his faith, but he sought to impose it upon these young men.

Though Shadrach, Meshach, and Abednego had favored positions in the king's administration, they held fast to their faith and refused to bow down. When the king saw their disobedience to the royal command, he offered them a second chance; they refused. In his anger, King Nebuchadnezzar had them thrown into the furnace. The furnace was so hot that those who did the deed were burned alive. Then, while in the fire, something happened—the boys were not burned. In fact, the king saw four bodies moving about where there had originally been three. When the king had them taken from the fire, Shadrach, Meshach, and Abednego were without a mark. It was at this point that the king abandoned his idol and declared the God of the Hebrews to be the true and living God.

There are some great lessons to be learned from this text and the incident with the fiery furnace. These lessons will help guide us spiritually in the twenty-first century. This text is really about the nature of faith: what it can expect, what it must do, and what it will produce. The people of God have to be ready, as Jude wrote, "… to contend for the faith that was once for all entrusted to the saints" *(Jude 1:3, NIV)*. We have to be ready for the battle that is coming. It will be a war over beliefs—beliefs about God, humanity, life, sin, death, hope, and faith. We must be able to hold our own. We must know in whom we believe and what we believe. The apostle Paul was correct when he wrote, "That we henceforth be no more children, tossed to and fro, and carried about with every wind of doctrine, by the sleight of men, and cunning craftiness, whereby they lie in wait to deceive" *(Ephesians 4:14, KJV)*. We are in the midst of difficult times, and we need a faith that can survive the furnace.

That is why the promises of God are ordered so as to give us the faith that we need not just to survive the flames but to thrive in the midst of them. God promises us that we can walk—and thrive—in the fire. God is not so limited that all he can do is keep us going in adversity. He is so powerful that he will empower us to *thrive* in the midst of distress. He will prepare a table for us in the very presence of our enemies and force them to watch us eat! Where our adversaries thought they would delight in our destruction, they will see how God delights in us!

## PITFALLS OF THE TWENTY-FIRST CENTURY

One of the dangers of our current age is that we have abdicated critical thinking and have become willing to accept anything that is put before us. The whole sense of living by convictions has been replaced with living by expedience. We have forfeited our principles and are unwilling to make a belief system central in our lives. There is an increasing great divide between those who believe and those who do not. In government, society, commerce, and even in families, there is a widening rift between those who believe and those for whom the person of God is just an idea. Many of us who have beliefs are not willing to practice them; our words and our works are not acting in harmony.

Some of us want to make our own way. Just like King Nebuchadnezzar, idolatry allows us to shape our god in the form we want him to take. He then becomes the god of our expediency. We are not so brazen as to define the job, the career, the money, or the children as our gods, but our actions and our words stand to declare that we have put something else in place of the true God. We ask Jehovah to move off the throne so that the god of our making can reign.

Some of us just want to live easy and comfortable lives. We do not want all the stress or drama that has accompanied the lives of so many others. But the truth of the matter is that these struggles are inevitable. In fact, we do not have to go looking for trouble. The Adversary will bring the fight straight to us. He will challenge us to see if our faith is real and if our God is real. He will rise up in family and friends. He will try us at work. He will enter our thoughts. We are under attack, and the fight is coming to us.

Why? Because when we do take positions of faith we invite a

war. Evil wants all of the territory it can claim, and often our faith is in the way of its accomplishing that goal. Seeing us as a stumbling block, the Enemy determines that we must be removed and our witness publicly rebuked.

Many of us are under attack right now. There are people who are trying to get us to bow and bend to practices and ways that we know are not correct. They are our friends, and their friendship matters. The pressure is often intense, but we must stand firm for the things we believe in. When we sacrifice our convictions, we set the stage for the Enemy to attack us; our souls stand unguarded. All of us have been guilty of this, and even in the twenty-first century, we must be vigilant and ready to face the inevitable fire.

Each of us who accepts Jesus in our hearts as Savior and Lord will find that an inferno is always raging. Look at what will happen when we face the fire and the furnace. Daniel 3:22 tells us that those who put the three youths in the fire were burned to death. This is no minor fact. The king was so angry at their affront to him that he had the furnace heated seven times hotter than it should have been. In the process of venting his anger, he cost others their lives. Whenever we are facing the furnace of life, rest assured that there will be casualties. The Enemy is so determined to get us that he will sacrifice others just to destroy us.

Others aided King Nebuchadnezzar in his effort. Others took offense at their stance of faith. These men felt threatened by these three Hebrews, so they sought to destroy them. They made the king aware that these three had refused to bow. They were the plotters and the schemers behind the scene.

Once we take our stand, the firestorm begins. Shadrach, Meshach, and Abednego did not face death because they committed some indiscretion. They refused to bow to an idol! In other words, they were standing for the honor of God and their allegiance to God. Some of us get it wrong. The challenge that God is calling us to fight is the challenge to own and honor him. The battle is over who is God. It is the battle Moses entered with Pharaoh and his magicians. It is the Elijah battle on Mount Carmel. It is the battle of

Christ on Calvary. This is about acknowledging him when everything around us is in jeopardy. It is about being unapologetic for being a child of the King. Such behavior will earn us the fire.

## ADVENT OF THE TWENTY-FIRST CENTURY

In this new era, we must have convictions. Even as we turn the opening pages of the twenty-first century, there are many more new ideas bursting forth on the horizon. It will take people of conviction and purpose to move in a constant and planned direction. It will take people of courage to declare that some directions are not in our best interest. Our parents tried to do this when we were children, but that has been lost on subsequent generations and now everything is open to experimentation. The Bible cautions us against this, for it says, "There is a way that seemeth right unto a man, but the end thereof are the ways of death" *(Proverbs 16:25, KJV)*. This is the great danger that overhangs our new adventure. Will we be a people of conviction or expediency? What will guide our thinking and acting in this new millennium?

First, we cannot change to accommodate people. The text in Daniel 3:16-18 says that Shadrach, Meshach, and Abednego dialogued with the king but refused to back down. In fact, they told him that they knew their God was able to deliver them. They spoke boldly to power. Faith empowers us to speak boldly to the systems and agents of power that seek to divert our lives from the God-directed purpose. There is a need for people of faith to trust the truth they teach and put it on the line with a declaration of their beliefs. The three youths knew the cost of their declaration, but they were willing to pay it. The words of the apostle Paul ring true, "… and having done all, to stand" *(Ephesians 6:13, KJV)*.

Next we must remember that God will still grant us freedom when the Enemy puts us in a furnace. Daniel 3:25 says the teens were *walking* in the fire, unharmed. We must understand that God will burn the ropes and set us free in the flame. Most people are afraid of the flame, but God says that which was intended to harm us can become an instrument to bless us. The fire was intended to kill them, but God empowered them and gave them freedom in a death situation.

That same verse says that there was a *fourth person* walking with them in the furnace. God puts an ambassador in every place that we are subject to travel. Just as our nation sends ambassadors to every country with which we have dealings, God gives us ambassadors to empower us to handle our business. There are angelic ambassadors on our jobs, in our neighborhoods, in our churches, in our homes, and also in our furnaces. God puts heavenly agents with us in the flames because in places like the furnace we need to know that the Lord is with us. When the devil launches his best weapons, we need the assurance that the Lord has not left us. We know he is with us because of the words of Scripture, but God understands that there are moments when we need more than that—there are moments when we really need to feel his presence in a direct way. He is there at those times.

We need to be encouraged by this truth: Our faith will remain intact in the fire and in the furnace. "… So Shadrach, Meshach and Abednego came out of the fire, and the satraps, prefects, governors and royal advisers crowded around them. They saw that the fire had not harmed their bodies, nor was a hair of their heads singed; their robes were not scorched, and there was no smell of fire on them" *(Daniel 3:26-28, NIV)*. They exited the fire without even the smell of fire on them. Everything they took into the fire was intact. The ropes that held them were the only things that burned. Their clothes represented their faith, and their faith was intact! This scene tells us that even today the things the world will seek to do to us will not last. They will be burned up. Do not fret over the lies, the controversies, the innuendoes, the statements, the petty tricks, and the dirty deeds of the Adversary; they will not last. They will be burned in the fire. God will bring us out without a scratch, rescue us without a mark, and deliver us without a sign of struggle. That is because he is the true God. He is over all.

We must be willing to tell our story and stand for what we believe. Our faith will cause others to believe. When King Nebuchadnezzar saw with his own eyes that these three youths were unharmed, he gave an order that no ill word could be spoken about the God of the Hebrews. Their commitment to God and their steadfast determination to serve him caused others to come to know the Lord. This is serious business because when we are in the fire, we must monitor our behavior and be careful of our conversation. The Lord wants endurance *and* edification. He wants us to go through the flames in such a way that others are drawn to us. We must understand that our witness will cause others to watch us. When the centurion saw Jesus dying on the cross, he cried out, "Surely this man was the Son of God!" *(Mark 15:39, NIV).* The Master's actions on the cross convinced the soldier that he was indeed the Son of God. When we hold up under pressure and survive the worst taunts of the Adversary, we convince others that our God is God. More than that, he is the God who answers by fire!

King Nebuchadnezzar was so impressed that he gave each of the teens a major promotion. The very thing they thought was costing them everything gained them even more. They thought their faith was responsible for their descent, but it was causing them to ascend. When we are true to our faith, God has a way of bringing us out on top. He has a way of making us rise in spite of every opposition. Shadrach, Meshach, and Abednego let their faith govern their actions and, in the end, God exalted them. It is still true that God rewards the faithful. In fact, the Scriptures declare in Hebrews 11:6 that, "... he is a rewarder of them that diligently seek him." God is met through the faith of his people, and he rewards those who stand for his kingdom.

This is our season, and we must stand fast. This is our time, and we must be ready. The furnace is being heated; the fire is raging. But the Lord of the fire is with us. He will not leave us alone. Whatever comes our way, our faith must stand and be ready. We must contend for the faith. We must hold up the faith. We must believe that our God *is* God.

# 15

# THE VICTORIOUS CHRIST

When you were dead in your sins and in the uncircumcision of your sinful nature, God made you alive with Christ. He forgave us all our sins, having canceled the written code, with its regulations, that was against us and that stood opposed to us; he took it away, nailing it to the cross. And having disarmed the powers and authorities, he made a public spectacle of them, triumphing over them by the cross.

*—Colossians 2:13-15, NIV*

## PROMISE OF THE TWENTY-FIRST CENTURY

THE HISTORY OF THE WORLD was irrevocably changed by the appearance of a carpenter from Nazareth who died on a cross. Into a world order dominated by Rome and trained by Greece came a thirty-year-old man with a message of redeeming love whose name was Jesus Christ. Many centuries had passed since God gave the word to Abraham that from him would come a great nation, and many millennia had elapsed since Adam and Eve were created and driven out of the garden. Since that day of banishment, evil had been spreading its wings. Since that day, humanity had surrendered its priority position and had begun taking orders from the prince of darkness. Since that day, people had dreaded death and saw it as the final futility. There was a dark cloud hanging over the world. It was as if the entire world was waiting in anxious anticipation for some great move, some action on behalf of heaven that would once and for all turn the tide and restore the created balance.

During the time of Jesus, the Romans had extracted a high toll from the captive Israelis. Into the power play came the Zealots, a quasi-military group formed for the sole purpose of liberating Israel from Rome. The air was filled with the thought of a military battle, a final war, a cataclysmic upheaval that would cause Palestine to be a battleground. The world was expecting a military confrontation with guerrilla warriors against Roman generals, but the battle was not to be as anticipated. A war *was* about to begin, but it would be between the real combatants, heaven and hell. The war was about to begin, but it would not be on an earthly battleground, but rather on an old rugged cross—one solitary earthly figure facing and fighting the legion of unseen forces led by the prince of darkness—a battle raging in heaven and on earth between seen and unseen forces, between the creation and the Creator. One soldier steps forward to defend the entire human race against capitulation to the lord of the flies. One human being filled with the purposes of heaven and the Spirit of God comes forward to face the deceiver of the brethren. Those around him have absolutely no clue about what is happening. The universe is waiting with baited breath for the outcome. Hell is mobilized with its strongest forces, and heaven has declared that the favor of God is upon him.

We know Jesus of Jerusalem as the prophet of Nazareth, but he is also the champion of the Lord's forces and the defender of the faithful. He is, in reality, more than just a man. He is a man with a mission, a man with determination, a man with commitment, and a man with resolve. These are his human attributes for such a contest, but there is something more than this at work in this man. Those things in and of themselves are enough to get him on the field, but they are not enough to guarantee victory. Flesh and blood are no match for the spirit of the ungod. There is more that is needed, and Jesus has it. He was and is the Son of the Living God. The power of God that was at work in the creation of the world is also at work in him. In him is the fullness of the Godhead. He is the power of God, the Word, the declaration of the mind and thoughts of the Almighty. He is the ultimate power of speech: his word creates and destroys.

The world has been changed. Though we are still plagued by the residue of evil in our midst and its dominion over our lives, its power has been broken and its gates have been destroyed. Though we did not and still do not fully comprehend the ramifications of this victory, one thing is for sure: On Easter morning, the Lord Jesus Christ rose from the dead, and he rose with all power in his hand. All the forces of heaven and hell knew that he was the *victorious Christ!* All that we need for life and liberty has been tendered to us by the transaction on Calvary. There Jesus Christ took care of everything and the charges were dropped against us. On Calvary, every issue was settled and every claim exposed. On Calvary, the Lord revealed once and for all who he is and the power that is at work in him. At Calvary, we saw the fullness of the Godhead bodily and the image of the invisible God. On Calvary, he triumphed over every foe and spoiled the kingdom of darkness. He is undeniably the victorious Christ!

Though the Lord defeated the power of hell itself, its imps are still seeking to imprison humanity because some do not have the knowledge necessary to fight back. Some do not know that Christ has won the victory and has vanquished the power of darkness. The words of Hosea 4:6 are still true, "My people are destroyed for lack of knowledge...." It is the aim of the church and the mission of its ministry to bring to people not only the knowledge necessary to participate in the victory, but also to expose them to the God who has done this for them. It is the aim of the church to introduce them to the joy and excitement that he offers.

We are not standing alone on the battlefield facing insurmountable odds! We are not fighting solely with the support of our own efforts and intellect. We have not been left behind to defend the post by ourselves. We have been joined in the battle by none other than the one whose power defeated hell itself. He is there to remind our enemy that the hold has been broken. The deceiver's claims to us have been terminated. We are aligned with the victorious Christ. We are aided by the Lord of Life. He promises us that we are never, never alone in the struggle. In this spiritual war, we have the strength of the Lord Jesus Christ on our side.

## PITFALLS OF THE TWENTY-FIRST CENTURY

It is with this in mind that the apostle Paul wrote to the church at Colossae. He did not visit this city, but he wrote them a message that he hoped would help them throw out the Adversary. Colossae's problems were unique. The forces of evil had attacked them through what the Greeks called the "wisdom of the world." Paul earnestly implores them, "I tell you this so that no one may deceive you by fine-sounding arguments.... See to it that no one takes you captive through hollow and deceptive philosophy, which depends on human tradition and the basic principles of this world rather than on Christ" *(Colossians 2:4,8, NIV)*.

Colossae's version of strange teaching was indeed unique. The Gnostics, the intellectuals of their day, had come to this region and were teaching that Jesus Christ was not really human. They taught that he was some kind of spiritual being. Moreover, they also taught that the way to God was through knowledge. They sought to wed their Greek techniques with Christian teaching. They sought some sort of hybrid faith. They wanted to believe that the world had a say in the teachings of Jesus. This teaching combined both Jewish and pagan observances. This teaching pretended to improve upon the Gospel that had come from Paul. Practices were included within a philosophy in which angels played a leading role. They taught this hybrid faith, and many were led astray.

This false religion is still being promoted and practiced today. We seek to wed Christ with culture and smorgasbord the faith. We pick and choose and add and subtract until we have a religion we are comfortable with, which does not force us to make a choice. The Adversary does not want us to choose, because he wants to keep us on his payroll. He uses our insecurities and shortcomings as the doorkeeper who allows entry of his henchmen. These henchmen then proceed to ransack our peace of mind and rob us of our confidence. The prince of the air wants to cloud our vision and distort our thinking so that we see ourselves as alone and fatally flawed. He wants to discourage our forces so that we cannot take advantage of the victory Christ has already won.

Regardless of the people and the positions they hold, we have to be careful of enticing words. We must be careful of the conversations we allow in our lives. Many saints have been confused and even drawn off by the enticing words of others. Today there is a fascination with the New Age religions that stress "channeling" and "visioning." They teach that we are all gods and that we are divine. They teach false doctrine, and people race to hear their proponents speak. Our effort to be superior makes us prime targets for the Enemy's mind games. We want to feel as if we are more spiritual than others or that we have some corner on the revelation market. We fall into the same trap as Adam and Eve: We want to be God. Satan uses our errant desire to undo us and pull us away from our source of strength. He makes us go up against God so that we will have no confidence in the fact that God is standing with us. Eventually, the wisdom of the world crashes, and those who have followed it are left with the emptiness that false gods leave when they depart.

The body of Christ must be careful of enticing words. We hear so much that masquerades under the name of religion. It sounds good and right, but a careful inspection reveals that it is clanging brass and a tingling cymbal. We hear people use religion to push political agendas. Be careful of people who claim to love us but want capital punishment to wipe us out. Be leery of people who speak of God and decry abortion but will not adopt the babies they have forced to be born. Watch enticing words. We are drawn in by the lure of faith and caught by the hook of a political agenda. We must always watch from whose tables we eat. We must be careful of the tables of faith from which we feed.

Chapter 15

## ADVENT OF THE TWENTY-FIRST CENTURY

Everything is now new. As the apostle Paul declares in 2 Corinthians 5:17 *(KJV)*, the old ways have passed away: "... behold, all things are become new." Look again at Colossians 2:13-15 *(NIV)* and see what Christ has done for us:

- New life—"When you were dead in your sins ... God made you alive with Christ."
- New chance—"He forgave us all our sins ... "
- New standing—"(He) canceled the written code ... that stood opposed to us ..."
- New theology—"... he (nailed) it to the cross."

God gave us the resource to become new, and that resource is Jesus Christ, the Righteous One. The Lord defeated Satan with the very shame Satan tried to put on him. The forces of evil were not content to make the Master's life miserable. They wanted him broken and surrendered. They wanted him to prove, as had all before him, his inability to withstand the fiery darts of the devil. He wanted Jesus to show the Father that no creature could withstand the attack. He wanted Jesus to prove that all of us are frail and that we would rather serve evil than suffer for righteousness. When it came time for the assault, the scene looked grim. Jesus was betrayed by a friend, abandoned by his followers, ridiculed by leaders, rejected by a follower, and crucified on a cross. Even the cross itself was a symbol of shame.

Yet it was precisely the shame that was used to bring victory. The cross was to be the final straw that even this great Teacher could not overcome. In the providence of God, though, he turned the shame into a symbol. That which was used against the Master was reshaped into the symbol of our faith. It is the mark of all we believe. It is more than the symbol of his suffering; it is the symbol of our victory.

The Adversary lost his battle with Jesus when he tried to use shame. He will lose with us when we realize that the Victor of the shameful cross stands with us in our shame and has declared its power broken. In the story of the prodigal son found in Luke 15:11-32, the elder son is angered at the treatment the father shows the prodigal when he returns home. The elder son is angry that his profligate brother should seemingly be rewarded for his actions by the grand celebration his father is preparing. But the son's return from ruin is the very thing the father is celebrating. The father has turned the shame into a mark of distinction.

Many of us still carry the scars and the keloids of our mistakes and failures. Our shame is like the scarlet letter sewn onto our jacket. But these scars will be our passport into the lives others. We can use our stories to help and heal others. Our testimonies of what the Lord has done for us can be turned around to show what the Lord will do for others. Our shame and suffering become the tools that break the dark kingdom's hold on the lives of others who are wandering and seeking.

There is still a deeper truth that cannot be missed. Paul saw that, while we were dead, God made us alive. There can be no doubt that the Lord means for us to have victory. Jesus withstood the darts of the devil because he was committed to his purpose. He came to save, and he would not be deterred. The Lord was victorious because he took purpose and turned it into power. The purpose for which he came to this earth motivated him and kept him on tract; in doing so he turned it into power. When we let the purpose for which we fight become so significant that we do not mind begging God to aid us, that purpose becomes power. The problem with so many of us is that we allow the Devil to frustrate our purpose. We let the Adversary create havoc with that which is important. The Evil One knows that if we become focused and committed, God will turn that commitment into a spiritual power that will enable us to stand against all the wiles of the Devil. When we become so focused that the only things we see are our mission and our Master, there will be no stopping us.

This is the whole history of the church. This is the record of successful people. This is the way to spiritual victory. What makes this different from twenty-first-century humanism and New Age spiritualism is that the fulfillment of purpose becomes linked to the power of the Lord. Jesus becomes the equalizer in the battle equation. In fact, he tips the scales on our behalf. His commitment to victory and his winning of the battle makes him available to us for our struggle. In other words, we are not in the fight alone. He has become our helper. We can win because we have assistance from the One who has all power. We need not fear the fight. Cry out to the Lord! He will never leave the righteous forsaken. He will empower us with his power. We will receive what belongs to him. As it was in him, so it will be in us.

As we prepare to win our battles, we must remember that our greatest weapon is *love*. It is love that defeats the Adversary. When Jesus walked the earth, his message was that of love. At the cross, love was sent into the battle and became the ultimate weapon. There Jesus showed us that he wins battles by his Spirit, which is the spirit of love. We often think of love as petty sentimentality, but Jesus raises it to a new level. In the end, love does not show us weak and anemic; it marches onto the battlefield as the most potent force in the universe. It is love that the Lord uses to defeat the anger and hate of Calvary. It is our ability to maintain love that cripples every effort launched against us.

Face the Adversary with the love of God! When we stand in every situation aware that somehow God has a plan, our love for him and our love for his plan will not let us go down. He is with us, and we will stand. Every time we win a battle, we make a spectacle of the one who tried to break us. Every time we stand up under pressure, we make a spectacle of the one who tried to destroy us. Every time we hold our head up, refuse to accept defeat, and start the battle all over again, we make a spectacle of the one who thought we were finished. Trust and rest assured that God did not bring us this far to leave us now. *He will stand with us. The victory is ours!*